W9-CTN-153

AMERICAN HOUSE NOW

AMERICAN HOUSE NOW

CONTEMPORARY ARCHITECTURAL DIRECTIONS

SUSAN DOUBILET AND DARALICE BOLES

UNIVERSE

First published in the United States of America in 1997
by UNIVERSE PUBLISHING
A Division of Rizzoli International Publications, Inc.
300 Park Avenue South
New York, NY 10010

00 / 10 9 8 7 6 5 4

Library of Congress Catalog Card Number: 97-061189

Design by Group C Inc New Haven/Boston (BC, FS, AT, CW)

Printed in Italy

CONTENTS

SUSAN DOUBILET   DARALICE BOLES

AMERICAN...

The twenty-four houses included in this book were chosen because of their design excellence and because they represent "now," that is, the state of architectural design at this time. They were all conceived by architects living and working in North America, though a number of these architects were born and raised elsewhere; all but four of the projects are sited in the United States. The one project located not in the Americas but in Japan is designed by a young, internationally known American architect, and it represents the export and adaptation of American ideas, a result of growing globalization.

Despite the diversity of the architects' national backgrounds, their designs demonstrate a number of American characteristics. Indeed, one of these characteristics is diversity itself, clearly seen in the variety of architectural expression fostered by a climate of tolerance in the United States. Those architects who migrated to these shores did so in part because of a perceived American openness to new ideas, and in so doing contributed to the very plurality that attracted them in the first place. One part of this plurality is the pursuit of opposite ideals simultaneously: the instinct for bigness and the appreciation of smallness, for example, or the drive toward increased sophistication and the adulation of naive youth.

VARIETY OF EXPRESSION

In America, "how it was done," while of interest and import, has never been a formula for "how to do it." The houses in this volume all share a point of origin. They subscribe to the general tenets of Modernism, that is, they are abstract in form, reflect some aspects of the true nature of their function and structure, and eschew traditional forms and ornamentation; moreover, they were all designed during the same time period. Yet they differ markedly from one another. On one end of the scale are the white, sculptural forms of Richard Meier—cerebral and unviolated. At the other end is the rugged expressionism of Eric Owen Moss. And along the way are almost as many directions as houses shown.

BIGNESS

The American urge to "do your own thing" is as much a function of space as attitude. The country's large size and relatively low density of population encourage an expansiveness of manner, which translates directly into design: big sites, rare in other countries, can still be found in the United States, and the houses on them spread out, both literally and expressively. John Lautner's Goldstein Residence celebrates that American-style expansiveness by its sheer bravado. The house seems to be all roof and no walls; furthermore, its inhabitants can afford, because of the site's size, to be separated from the outdoors only by glass, even as they shower. Richard Meier expresses the land's bigness differently; his Grotta House surveys its broad meadow site calmly, majestically, almost haughtily. And the bigness of Gwathmey Siegel's Pacific Palisades House is literal: it is big—very, very big—and it demonstrates how luxury at this time is not a matter of ornamentation but of generous spaces.

PRAGMATISM

At the same time, a number of the houses demonstrate another American characteristic: pragmatism. Americans tend to face and solve problems directly: "get the job at hand done and get on with it" is the impulse. American architects tend to take only what they need from passing stylistic movements. As one example, American architects adapted the aesthetics but not the social program of the early Modern movement originating in Europe. As another example, the high-tech movement, which elevates a building's technological solutions to its major aesthetic expression, has never really caught on in America as it has, say, in England. In North America, the closest kin to high-tech buildings can be found in those designs that appropriate structural and mechanical systems and materials developed for various building types. The Park Road House by Canadian Don McKay is just such a building; it amalgamates a structural system normally used for commercial buildings, materials from both residential and industrial sources, and a spatial organization based on the adaptable nineteenth-century farmhouse. This hybrid design has no manifesto behind it; decisions were made pragmatically, because they responded to one particular set of conditions.

Pragmatists are rarely purists; they tend rather toward inclusivity. The Collective Housing by Fernau & Hartman demonstrates this ad hoc, "have it your way" approach. Because the design process was inclusive, the form of the buildings has an open-ended quality. A variety of elements responding to specific needs was added

7

to the basic buildings during the design and will continue to be added over the years as the residents' needs change.

Another aspect of "pragmatism" is the converse of bigness. This is the "enough is enough" approach, part of the American character. Neither the Croffeads, who were Clark & Menefee's clients, nor Stanley Saitowitz's clients, the McDonalds, wanted to pay for (in the words of Mrs. Croffead) "rooms sitting around waiting to be used." At the same time, the expression of each of these houses is big; the Croffeads' possesses a certain monumentality, the McDonalds' an expansiveness that reaches up and out to sun and sea.

Finally, American pragmatism plays out for some architects in the urge to invent new uses of materials or new gadgets. Both can be found in the Blades Residence, with its flamed formwork and elaborate fireplace pulley system; in the Landes House, with its mechanical sun screens; and in the Goldstein Residence, with its corner windows that retract above a sheer precipice.

PURITY

Just as pragmatism exists in American design, so does its opposite: the desire for "purity." In part, this is due to Americans' strong love for newness. In America's Modern houses, clarity is achieved through hard and careful work, which reduces complex ideas to their essence and ensures that the design message is unmistakable. Richard Meier's designs are prime examples of purity; Carlos Zapata's Landes House is shiny and sharp-edged; Arquitectonica's Casa los Andes is composed of clearly differentiated, brightly colored elements.

At the same time, purity is related to wholesomeness, and is thus connected to another American preoccupation, the adulation of youth. Youth represents the most natural, unspoiled state of being; yet as the permanent object of desire, it cannot remain perpetually untainted. In America at least, youth has not remained so, and the architectural expression of both sides of the coin—fresh, brightly hued, firm forms fused to a glamorous, sophisticated lifestyle—forms the basis of Arquitectonica's work.

HOUSE...

It is the great American dream to own a single-family house. The house on its own defined piece of land serves as moated castle, the place to withdraw from the world. And house ownership is the emblem of success, proof of having made it. For most Americans, the requisite house is located in the suburbs, and for most, its look is predictable. Despite the stated ideal of individuality, the true desire of most people is conformity: in the east, the coveted house, tiny or very large, is likely to be Colonial; and in the west, California ranch.

But in a small percentage of cases, the house becomes a vehicle of personal expression for both the clients and the architect. For the clients, the drive to create and possess a house truly of their own is both Eros and Thanatos: to craft a nest where one can live and live out one's life, both stimulated and sheltered by the house's embrace.

For the architect, the house is both talisman and testing ground. The house as design laboratory for the architect is not only a truism, it's a fact. Despite changes in family structure, leisure time, and household technology, the basic diagram remains essentially unaltered in two hundred years of American architectural history. Because the program is so thoroughly known, architects are free to give full range to their creativity. The nearly sacred simplicity of the house also makes it the last building type for which an architect can sometimes exercise almost complete design control, free of the often pernicious influence of developers, cost managers, hydra-headed client committees, and government bureaucrats.

The house, then, is the repository and fulfillment of dreams and fantasies on both sides—architect and client. Its cultural importance in America cannot be overstated: in a nation that emphasizes choice and individual expression, prizes originality, and exhibits an intense interest in psychoanalysis, the house is the final apotheosis of personality.

At the same time, many architects have concluded that individual expression in architecture must be merged with collective cultural myths and memories. Antoine Predock, for example, goes well beyond pragmatic responses to the environment to incorporate spiritually satisfying myths about the special qualities of the land. He designs buildings that respond physically to the environment of the American

Southwest and aesthetically to the need for spiritual ties to the earth: the White Residence reminds us of a simple adobe structure but is far more sophisticated. Machado and Silvetti, in their Concord House, assemble a number of room types that, while abstracted, remind us of traditional architecture. The overall composition manages not only to recount the architectural history of the semirural site, but to create a psychological portrait of their knowledgeable clients and their extensive architectural experiences. Steven Holl, both in the Berkowitz-Odgis House and the Makuhari Housing, finds literary constructs that he weaves into the expression of his buildings. And in California, the firms of RoTo and Morphosis base their designs on highly cerebral themes, among them the myth of mathematical perfection.

NOW...

Inevitable confusion attends the term "Modern architecture." In one sense, it stands for a period in architectural history running roughly from the 1920s, with the formation of the Bauhaus in Germany, to the 1970s, when Postmodern theorists declared the style dead. In another sense, the word "modern" means of the moment; thus to be "modern" in the late 1990s is to seek to express our time, *this* time.

In some ways, architecture today is both Modern and modern. In others, classic Modernism is indeed dead, as is classical Postmodernism. But it is closer to the truth to say that the best qualities of both Modernism and Postmodernism have been distilled and merged. What you will see in these pages is clearly not Postmodern, though it could not have happened without the Postmodern movement. Similarly, these houses do not deny their Modern lineage, though they represent a new generation that is still learning from the mistakes of history.

To understand where we are, then, it is necessary to take a brief look at where we've been. In 1919, architect Walter Gropius founded the Bauhaus school in Weimar, Germany, following a period in which historical styles—primarily Classical or Gothic—were applied purely as decoration to buildings constructed in new materials, including cast iron, steel, and poured concrete. Gropius and his followers insisted that a new aesthetic, free of ornamentation, be created to express these new materials as well as a new age.

Gropius emigrated to the United States at the start of World War II, followed by Mies van der Rohe. By then, however, the basis for a specifically American Modernism was already in place, defined by an exhibition at the Museum of Modern Art in 1932 that was entitled *The International Style.* The show stripped Modernism of the social agenda that had accompanied the style's development in Europe. Its curators, Henry-Russell Hitchcock and Philip Johnson, concentrated exclusively on aesthetics, codifying the elements that make a building Modern, such as the horizontal strip window, the flat roof, and the free plan.

By the 1970s, Modernism in America had degenerated into a sterile, repetitive formula in the hands of some architects and excessively arcane object-making in others'. The infamous glass and steel box, justified by the Modernist mantra "form follows function," was generally acknowledged as environmentally inefficient and urbanistically inhumane. The alternative, a muscular, rough-concrete Modernism developed in the 1960s and called the New Brutalism, was just that to the public—brutal. Attempts in the late 1950s and '60s to revive the social and political intentions of early Modernism ended with the demolition of the Pruitt-Igoe housing project in St. Louis in 1972.

The aesthetic limitations and sociological failings of American Modernism were easily targeted by a new generation of architects who absolutely rejected the idea of absolutes in architecture. These Postmodernists preached a looser, more inclusive approach that embraced historical precedent, regional styles and materials, and context. Not coincidentally, the rise of academic Postmodernism in America paralleled a grass-roots movement for historic preservation. Beginning with Robert Venturi's *Complexity and Contradiction in Architecture* (1966) and Robert A. M. Stern's *New Directions in American Architecture* (1977), an alternative to Late Modern architecture began to emerge, first in words, then, less satisfactorily, in buildings.

American culture is seldom free of ambivalence towards tradition: we are still in some sense a young nation, and see ourselves as youthful, brash, and inventive; on the other hand, we cling to our (relatively new) traditions as the source of our authenticity and importance. The Postmodern movement played to this peculiarly American insecurity twice over, in the use of architectural history as a treasure trove of signs and symbols intended to confer status on the architecture in which it appeared, and in an ironic preference for popular culture over high art. These two attitudes became in effect two camps within the Postmodern movement: one searching for precedent in vernacular architecture—strip malls and main streets— and the other paging through the history of "serious" architecture. A rigorous few advocated a return to true Classicism, the style of early America.

With astonishing speed, Postmodern historicism was co-opted by corporate architects and their clients, just as Modern architecture had been. Fueled by a flush American economy, the building boom of the early and mid-1980s produced a rash of "high-rises with hats," that were Postmodern in only the most superficial way. At the same time, some of the key figures moved in more personal directions, as did, for example, Michael Graves, who began his career as a Modernist and then developed a distinctive, Classically derived style that has been widely and badly copied by many architects.

While both historicist and vernacular Postmodernism burnt out quickly, one strain survived, minus the Postmodern label. The so-called Five Architects proposed a return to early Modernism. The role model of these architects was not Mies van der Rohe, but Le Corbusier. Two of the five, Charles Gwathmey and Richard Meier, are included in the volume, and their work proves that pure, sculptural form is still powerful.

So where are we now? Recoiling equally from the meanness of Late Modern architecture and the excess of Postmodernism, architects in the late 1990s are freer than their predecessors in either camp—free to combine the best of both and to introduce their own new elements. The watchwords of this age are appropriation and hybridization—pluralism without overt historicism. While postwar Modernism aimed for an unachievable objectivity and universality, today's more subjective and varied modernity is based in a common architectural language that is abstract but neither prescriptive nor universal in application. Moreover, many of the architects whose work is shown in this volume seek to recover aspects of architecture that were lost or obscured in American Modernism in the second half of this century, such as the importance of procession and movement through built space, the distinction between public and private domains, the tactile or material side of architecture, and a love of technological invention and display. At the same time, contextualism, a basic tenet of Postmodernism, is reflected in the attention paid to built or natural surroundings.

These architects draw their inspiration from a wide range of sources. Architects Frank Lloyd Wright, Irving Gill, Charles Eames, Louis Kahn, Luis Barragan and Frank Gehry are aesthetic mentors to many. The houses by Morphosis and RoTo draw upon the strong tradition of abstraction in American art and architecture, while the work of Frank Israel celebrates that vernacular icon, the ranch house. Machado and Silvetti practice a kind of Postmodern Modernism that draws on both vernacular and academic traditions; Donald McKay combines an industrial loft and a farmhouse. Antoine Predock draws on American landscape; Steven Holl culls inspiration from American literature.

While these architects in no way represent a common school of architecture, their work betrays a series of shared preoccupations that are fundamentally "modern" if not "Modernist." Dynamism, spatial energy, complexity in plan, and instability are the means by which some, such as Zapata, RoTo, and Morphosis, express what it signifies to live at the end of the twentieth century. Other architects, such as W. G. Clark and Stanley Saitowitz, seek not to reflect contemporary life but to provide a refuge from it. There is in many of these designs the desire to test limits of gravity, of material, and of composition, and the urge to create a building that is felt as much as seen. Finally, these architects seek not to solve universal problems but to focus instead on the personal, the idiosyncratic, the particular needs of a given client, the specific possibilities of a given place.

These points tie together otherwise diverse, though never contradictory, designs. The very variety of responses to the simple problem of the *House* identifies the work as *American*, and *Now*. ■

GWATHMEY SIEGEL & ASSOCIATES ARCHITECTS

PACIFIC PALISADES RESIDENCE PACIFIC PALISADES, CA

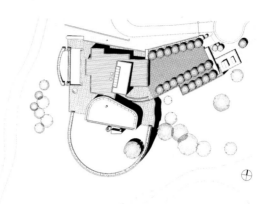

Charles Gwathmey was one of several young architects who, in the late 1960s, turned away from the dry and mechanistic path that Late Modern architecture had taken— away, that is, from design approached as the demonstration of an organizational system—and returned to the expression of the individual problem at hand. The architects used as their framework the theory and forms of the early Modernist movement, especially as articulated by Le Corbusier, and saw each individual problem as worthy of minute and intimate response. Their first commissions were houses, and houses remain important repositories of their creative energies, even as their practices have grown. (Among Gwathmey Siegel's best-known works, for example, is the addition to the Guggenheim Museum in New York City.) Of that innovative group from the '60s, Gwathmey has proven to be most adaptable and least identifiable, as he reshapes his still recognizably Modernist forms to suit the particular conditions of each commission.

The long glazed front of the curved limestone pavilion faces expansive ocean views.

The 18,000-square-foot Pacific Palisades Residence, designed for a film producer and director and located near the top of Malibu Canyon, consists of two distinct parts, reflecting the dual nature of the site. On one side is a basically rectilinear piece, as stern as the canyon wall from which it emerges. On the other is a free-form pavilion, reaching for the ocean and the infinite horizon. It is the very particularity of the design, responding to its specific, dramatic site and the glamorous professions of the clients, that marks this house as a Gwathmey Siegel work.

Metallic elements—stair rails and brise soleil screen—modulate the limestone pavilion's main facade.

The main entrance is placed at the juncture between the curved pavilion and the rectilinear block behind it.

The curved limestone pavilion contains the major rooms on three levels. Taking advantage of spectacular ocean views are the living and dining areas on the mid-level entry floor, game rooms and covered terrace beneath, and master bedroom above. This pavilion is both relaxed in form, like an ocean-tossed stone or seashell, and highly refined. Its contents—the free-form rooms and the people who use them—are simultaneously nestled by the solid curved wall and nudged toward the precipice, represented by the seventy-foot-long, two-story glazed wall. Related to the work of Le Corbusier are the cubist piano shape of the curve and the stainless steel *brise soleil* screen shading the long window wall.

Hugging the canyon wall is the "support building," containing guest bedrooms, a large screening room, archival storage, and office space. Rectilinear and stucco-clad, it is the sober half of this architectural partnership.

Both dining room and living room are embraced by the textured limestone wall.

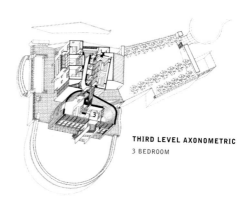

THIRD LEVEL AXONOMETRIC
3 BEDROOM

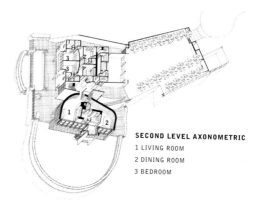

SECOND LEVEL AXONOMETRIC
1 LIVING ROOM
2 DINING ROOM
3 BEDROOM

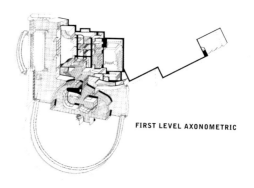

FIRST LEVEL AXONOMETRIC

The main interior staircase provides dramatic views of the canyon. The master bedroom (opposite), shown with its dressing room, takes in ocean views.

The house represents, to a large degree, the classical Modernist approach for which the New York firm has long been known—dignified, calm, reserved in color, generous in size but not sybaritic in materials. Each part of the house constitutes a recognizable Modernist building type. But in other ways the house intentionally violates some of the traditional Modernist design canons. The two disparate building parts seem casually assembled and collage-like, with neither one formally deferring to the other. In fact, the entry, whose placement in either structure would identify that structure as the dominant one, is located at the juncture between the two parts. The motivations for these design "violations" are twofold: to respond directly and intimately to the site and to express a looseness and an openness to future, unpredictable developments. ■

The restrained Modernist guest pavilion overlooks the pool.

MACK ARCHITECTS

The house is broken down into a series of separate volumes distinguished from each other and the surrounding landscape by a palette of bright colors.

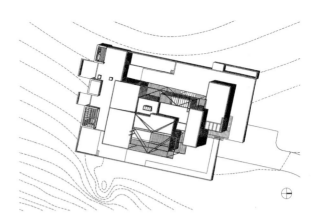

Two parts Vienna and one part California, or perhaps the reverse, Mark Mack is as comfortable quoting Austrian modernist Adolf Loos as he is Mexican regionalist Luis Barragan. The Austrian architect, who has spent most of his professional life in California, finds common ground between these extremes in an emphasis on the pure, archaic elements of architecture—structure and materials—that transcend style or period. In an age that values complexity, his work is almost countercultural in its straightforward simplicity.

All the elements that have come to be identified with Mack's approach, and especially his residential designs, are present in the Stremmel House. The various residential functions are housed in separate Loosian volumes or blocks whose vibrant colors are selected to contrast with each other and the surrounding landscape, in the manner of Barragan. At the same time, the actual architecture appears more attenuated than is usual for Mack, who responds here to the specific requirements of this particular client, a gallery owner whose collection of modern art required large amounts of uninterrupted wall space, eighteen- to twenty-four-foot ceilings and the careful monitoring of daylight.

Windows—typically treated by Mack as punched openings in a solid masonry wall—have been pushed to the corners to maximize hanging space. This shift has the effect of making the blocks appear less solid. The overarching trellis is made of thin steel members to accommodate long spans. The result is altogether more elegant and identifiably Modern than is customary for Mack, whose work has been termed Neo-primitive for its elemental, astylar quality.

Public and private spaces in this house-cum-museum are strictly separated in a manner more European than American. The public living/dining galleries take on the character of a loft or warehouse, complete with off-the-shelf storefront windows. The south-facing bedrooms, which together with the kitchen and family room wrap a private courtyard and lap pool, are more intimate, with lower ceilings and warmer finishes.

Although large at 7,000 square feet, the house makes as little a mark as possible on the nine acres of fragile desert that surround it. All construction is confined to a concrete plinth pushed into the earth to the west, where a wall completes the courtyard and protects it from prevailing winds. The decision to distinguish architecture from landscape is evident in the strictly orthogonal plan and section, which is all right angles and no curves. The trellis and an L-shaped reflecting pool at the entrance mark the boundaries of habitation.

The second-floor study is a high vantage point above the living room. Off-the-shelf storefront windows provide dramatic views of the surrounding desert.

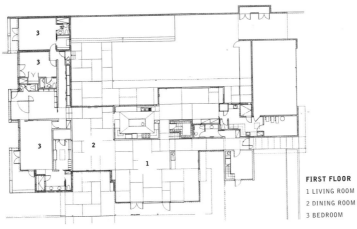

FIRST FLOOR
1 LIVING ROOM
2 DINING ROOM
3 BEDROOM

At the same time, within the house, the line between outside and in is blurred. Outdoor materials such as corrugated metal ceilings and concrete floors are used indoors. Every room in the house has direct access to the outdoors in a plan that recalls courtyard houses in the Southwest and other hot spots around the world.

This appreciation and appropriation of a traditional house type ties Mack to others on the fringes of mainstream Modernism who also mixed Modern and vernacular models. Not surprisingly, his list of favorite architects includes Scandinavian Gunnar Asplund and Slovenian Jože Plečnik, whose work, like Mack's, explores the seam between the universal and the particular, the balance between rational and intuitive.■

High ceilings and corner windows maximize hanging space for the owner's collection of contemporary art.

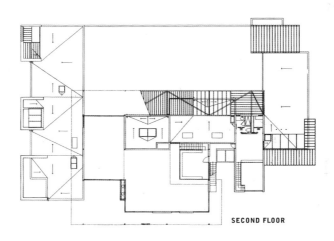

SECOND FLOOR

The light steel trellis unifies separate building blocks and adjacent outdoor courtyards.

The house sits on a plinth nestled into the gently sloping site. The rear courtyard is protected by a long masonry wall.

HARIRI & HARIRI

In some buildings, such as this harmonious lakefront cottage in Ontario's Algonquin Park, natural materials and a simple pitched roof convey the impression of a traditional building. Only a few gleaming elements in this house—the stainless steel chimney, the marble free-form hearth, the corrugated metal stair cabin—are overt reminders of the sleek Modernism for which its architects are known. In fact, a closer look reveals the building's basic Modernist design premise, which helped organize but not overwhelm the natural feel the clients sought.

The clients had two principal requests. Paramount was their desire to continue their family's seventy-year experience on this very site—relaxed, unpretentious, in concert with nature and with the simple cottage architecture in the area. In addition, the clients

The new wood-clad building, a long rectangle with a pitched roof, is tied to the original A-frame house by a sweeping cedar deck.

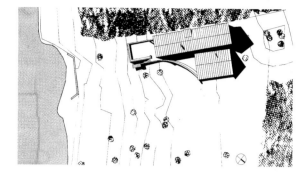

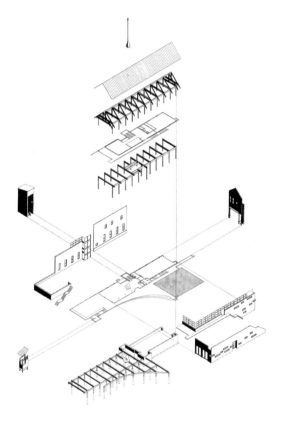

asked that the ordinary wood A-frame house existing on the lot be retained and expanded to accommodate their needs for more space.

The architects' solution was to design a separate new building only three feet away from the existing cottage, creating a two-building complex unified by a commodious wood deck. The new piece, 2,500 square feet in area, contains the living room on the main floor, with boat storage in the rear, and the master bedroom suite and reading room on the second floor. The existing house was gutted to accommodate the kitchen and dining room for the whole family, as well as bedrooms for children and guests.

Both new part and old were "nudged," architecturally, to respond to each other. The existing building was rendered more dignified: its fake shutters were removed, its pink trim paint was stripped, and its asphalt shingled roof was replaced by galvanized steel panels. The new building repeats the wood finishes and the pitched roof of the existing house, while incorporating Modernist themes.

First among the new piece's Modern aspects is its overall massing, as a hundred-foot-long, two-story bar building. Second is its disposition on the deck, which separates the building from nature and underscores its abstract, manmade quality. And third is the design of the facades, each different from the others and thereby revealing the relative

The horizontal windows alongside the deck are inspired by the pattern of birch bark (opposite).

independence of surface and structure. On the upper level of the lakefront facade, privacy was not an issue, permitting the use of large, sweeping windows to take advantage of the inspiring views. The west side has vertical windows responding to the stand of trees into which it nestles. And the east wall, which forms a backdrop for the most public part of the deck, has inventive horizontal strip windows inspired by the pattern of birch bark.

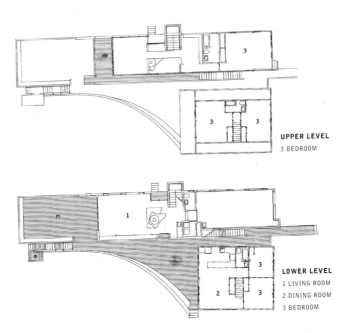

UPPER LEVEL
3 BEDROOM

LOWER LEVEL
1 LIVING ROOM
2 DINING ROOM
3 BEDROOM

The stainless-steel chimney, open free-form granite hearth, and corrugated metal stair cabin are gleaming Modern touches within this predominantly woodsy cottage.

The New York architects attribute some of the qualities of their design to their Iranian background, in addition to their architectural training at Cornell University. A unity of materials is common in Iranian buildings; here, the house employs red western cedar both inside and out, white maple flooring, and a few galvanized metal elements. The pervasive presence in Iran of beautiful pedestrian bridges made a lasting impression on the architects; here, the deck bridges the two parts of the house. And finally, the perspective of the architects as outsiders enables them, they feel, to identify certain essential qualities of North American building types; in this case, those of the wood cottage by the lake. ▪

The upper level reading room (opposite) takes full advantage of the charming lake views. A bridge connects the reading room to the master bedroom.

DONALD McKAY AND COMPANY

PARK ROAD HOUSE TORONTO, ONTARIO

From the street, this house in a sedate Toronto neighborhood is somewhat star-tling: it boasts uncontextual metallic panels and an elaborate metal entrance structure. Still, these details are mitigated by the reassuringly bland brick box that forms most of the house's street presence. Together, these divergent pieces give a hint of the themes that the house brings together. The design is based on the organization of the nineteenth-century Ontario farmhouse, but it is built like a twentieth-century commercial loft building and uses materials developed for industrial purposes. Homespun meets high tech; previously exclusive mindsets are blended into one hybrid form.

It was entirely appropriate that the Park Road House be envisioned as a farm-house. Serving not only as the architect's family residence but also as his art dealer wife's adjunct gallery and reception space, it encompasses, like the farmhouse, a cottage industry. Also, like the farmhouse, it must adapt to private and semi-commercial uses. Like the nineteenth-century farmhouse, whose four-square brick core was surrounded by partially enclosed porches used for cooking in the summer, canning in the fall, and playing in the winter, the 6,400-square-foot Park Road House's masonry core is wrapped at its rear by a translucent envelope, creating the appearance of kit-of-parts flexibility and reflecting the multiple functions within.

The size and brick cladding of the house's core resemble the neighboring houses, but the metal entrance bridge and corrugated metal cladding of the entrance/bedroom wing reflect the house's unusual nature.

45

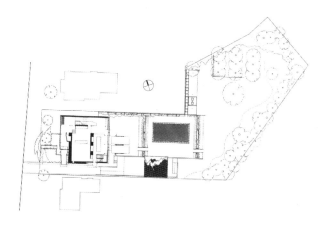

Aluminum mesh screens and steel awnings provide sun shading at the back of the house.

It was not appropriate, however, that the house look like a stolid farmhouse; it had to project a sophisticated, artistic image, in keeping with the avant-garde art it displays and the lifestyle of the artists it promotes. To achieve this imagery, the architect appropriated methods and materials generally associated with the high-tech movement. He crossed the divide between industrial design and residential architecture to choose corrugated aluminum panels commonly used to clad truck trailers. Aluminum mesh panels and steel awnings provide not only sun-shading but suavity as well.

And finally, the building systems were chosen for practicality. A large building volume was needed for big receptions; environmental conditions had to be controlled precisely to suit the artwork displayed. These requirements were most easily achieved by using commercial building methods. The steel frame, for example, with steel stairs and timber floor deck, is the type used commonly for modern office buildings in the 1950s and '60s.

The informal living room on the second floor (above) overlooks the dining area (opposite), from which it can be closed by a large sliding door. This second floor and the third-floor master bedroom suite (above top) constitute the family's private zone.

The house's ground floor, which holds a full-size commercial kitchen (above) and large, adaptable entertainment spaces, is built for hosting hundreds of people at a time. The third floor (opposite) provides private refuge space.

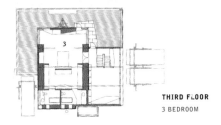

THIRD FLOOR
3 BEDROOM

SECOND FLOOR
1 LIVING ROOM
3 BEDROOM

FIRST FLOOR
1 LIVING ROOM
2 DINING ROOM

While high-tech architecture assumed heroic proportions earlier in this century and in other places, notably England (aiming to solve global housing problems, on the one hand, or forming a single, strong aesthetic, on the other), this house demonstrates a radical change in focus. The architect, who is also a furniture designer, professor, and writer, yoked ideas about technology to other architectural themes to create one suitable response to one set of requirements: hybrid architecture custom-designed to suit a hybrid lifestyle. ■

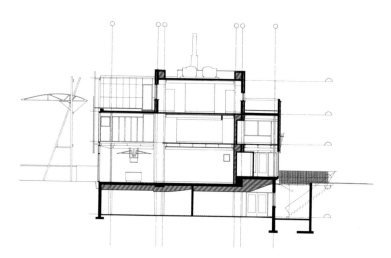

The steel, aluminum, and wood stairway is carefully designed, with every detail and connection clearly expressed.

FERNAU & HARTMAN ARCHITECTS

Three buildings—a central main lodge, a bedroom wing, and a workshop—are linked by pergolas and gently define a meadow within the redwood forest.

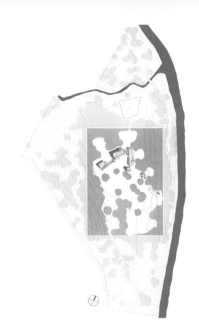

If you happened to be dropped into this casual group of buildings in a clearing in the woods, you might well mistake it for a long-standing summer camp recently freshened up, a camp located in a familiar forested area somewhere in America. So naturally does it fit into its setting, so comfortable is its appearance, and so much does it evoke, merely by its looks, the humming of the bees on a summer day, that it certainly doesn't feel like capital-A Architecture. It feels like, well, everyday.

It *is* the aura of day-to-day life that is intentionally reflected in this seemingly ad hoc complex. But this straightforward yet expressive piece of architecture reflects a very vital and varied, not a humdrum, day-to-day.

The project began as the result of a novel idea conceived by eleven middle-aged Californians: they would buy a piece of land and build a place where together they could eventually retire and share their old age, just as they have shared, as friends and neighbors, some of the minutiae of their younger and middle years. Being a group of inventive individuals

Adjacent to the entrance gate is the main lodge, which has communal rooms on the ground floor and bedrooms above.
The wide porch and stairs serve as bleachers for outdoor events; a stairway can be converted to a ramp if the need arises.

with a variety of opinions, they carefully chose architects who could work with them as a team. Furthermore, while they knew what they wanted for the near future, there was every likelihood that changes would be necessary over the years. The design had to be flexible. It also had to be moderate in price.

Berkeley architects Richard Fernau and Laura Hartman were selected, not only because their design process is based on teamwork, but because their actual designs reflect the cumulative approach. They begin with a strong basic idea of how to organize a scheme, and then append individual parts to the whole without obliterating the uniqueness of each part. They liken their work to the collage art of Robert Rauschenberg and Kurt Schwitters, in which "found objects" remain distinguishable even as they are brought into the overall composition.

The architects began the Collective Housing design by proposing simple, economical structures onto which add-ons would be incorporated. These structures—workshop, main lodge, and bedroom wing—were to be arranged casually around a meadow occurring within the redwood forest site. They were to be simple wedges economically

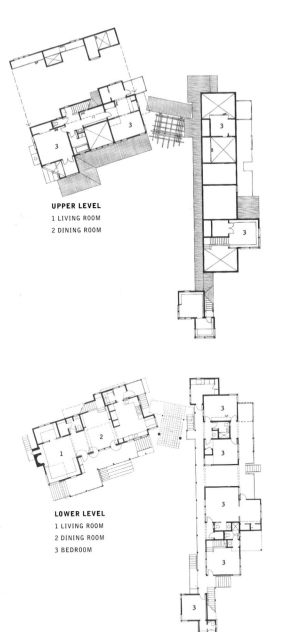

UPPER LEVEL
1 LIVING ROOM
2 DINING ROOM

LOWER LEVEL
1 LIVING ROOM
2 DINING ROOM
3 BEDROOM

sheathed in battened plywood and raised on stilts because the site is within a floodplain. As the design advanced, additional pieces were added to the wedges. Some add-ons consisted of responses to individual requests, such as the wish for a sleeping loft attached to a basic twelve by fifteen-foot bedroom. Some pieces were the result of a communal request, such as the need for a small library.

And thus the design progressed and was constructed. To retain the record of the design process, the basic wedges were stained dark green, the individually generated add-ons were colored red, and the communal add-ons were stained yellow. To promote a certain degree of togetherness (and coincidentally adding design variety), private and common areas were intermingled. The main lodge has bedrooms upstairs, and the bedroom wing has the laundry room at one end and the

The drawings show floor plans of the main lodge and bedroom wing. The bedroom wing (seen in the photographs) has a communal reading room, clad in yellow siding, at one end, and red-sided sleeping lofts along its rear wall.

two-story library tower at the other. Large porches accommodate outdoor group activities, and lofts provide extra sleeping space when extended family members visit. The three buildings, 6,000 square feet in all, are connected by pergolas that lightly define the meadow they surround. Already, a couple of years after the initial construction phase, small changes have been made: some unenclosed areas under the lofts have been walled in for more space. The design system, of course, easily incorporates these and future changes.

In just such a way has vernacular architecture come about throughout history. The best vernacular architecture has been the result of expediency and improvisation, shaped by intelligence, experience, and craft. Furthermore, say Fernau and Hartman, this type of design can be seen as the common person's Modernism: In keeping with mid-twentieth-century Modernist theory, functions are expressed; in keeping with the late twentieth-century drive toward realism, the process of design is revealed and the different parts are not regularized.■

A breakfast nook projects outward from the communal kitchen (above); a ladder leads up from the main lodge's second floor to sleeping lofts for guests (opposite).

LANDES HOUSE **GOLDEN BEACH, FL**

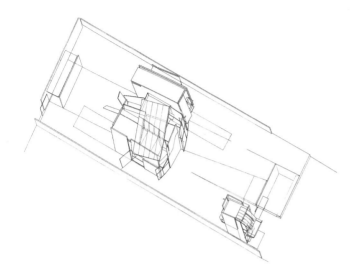

Carlos Zapata, who is young enough to have missed the fiercest of the "style wars" that dominated architectural education in the 1970s and '80s, is characteristically reluctant to discuss his Landes House in terms of style. Nevertheless, Landes—Zapata's first complete house—is a mature "signature" work by a relatively young architect from Ecuador who opened his own office in Florida only six years ago, and another more recently in Boston.

Although he is not allied to any particular school or philosophy, Zapata's approach to architecture, and the themes he chooses to explore, tie his work to that of other contemporary Neomodern or Deconstructivist architects, notably Zaha Hadid of London. Chief among these themes is the notion of "breaking the box" of Modern architecture. In the Landes House, no two walls meet at a right angle; instead, walls are handled as thin, dynamic planes angled in plan and section to suggest motion, instability, collision. Corners are frequently "erased" by the use of glass. Unexpected light breaks through cracks in the architecture. The handling of materials, such as the translucent onyx used at the entrance, is frequently sophisticated and original.

The entrance facade, which faces a busy highway, is largely closed and opaque; the garden facade (following pages) is more open and dynamic.

The house may appear more Futurist than Floridian; nevertheless, the new floor plan repeats almost exactly the footprint of a Spanish Colonial house torn down to make way for Zapata's design. Within this existing outline, the 6,200-square-foot main house is organized in a simple H, with the master suite, a study, and a gym in the southern block, and children's bedrooms above the dining room and kitchen in the northern block, joined by a double-height entry space and living spaces. The rooms themselves turn away from a busy highway that bounds the plot to the west; their fanlike organization allows all but one room to "touch" the ocean, a specific client request.

A fascination for the new, the untested, plays out both in structure (what holds the house together) and in detail (what the house holds). The cantilevered family room, for example, is secured by a pair of impossibly thin hanger rods; it soars out over the entry in a manner that is both exciting and frightening. The jagged copper sun scoop rising sharply above the main house is a structural and aesthetic tour de force. On one level, it solves the problem of daylight, admitting early morning and late afternoon light while screening harsher midday sun; on another, it gives the facade drama

The copper sun screen on the separate office/guest suite is hydraulically controlled.

The handling of structure and materials, from the dramatically cantilevered family room to the translucent onyx entry wall, reinforces a sense of dynamism and energy.

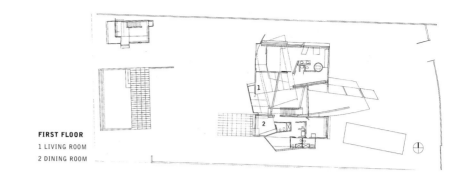

and dynamism. (Zapata worked closely with structural engineer William Faschan of Leslie E. Robertson Associates on the design of these and other details.) Similarly, the facade of the 630-square-foot guest house/office at the ocean's edge is shaped by a hydraulically controlled copper screen that moves up and down to shield curved glass windows.

These elements are both necessary and beautiful, crossing the line between architectural technology and aesthetic expression. In this regard, the Landes House is classically Modern: it adheres to the Modernist belief that functional invention and aesthetic innovation are one. ∎

The stair with its minimalist stainless steel banister appears suspended in the air.

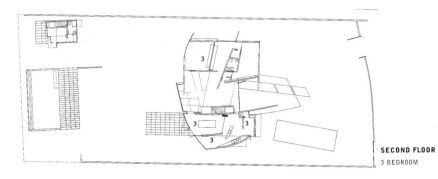

SECOND FLOOR
3 BEDROOM

TEIGER HOUSE SOMERSET COUNTY, NEW JERSEY

There is in every architect-designed house a tension or balance between what the architect brings to the project and what he or she finds there—in the place, the program, and the people whose lives and rituals the house will embody and encourage. Thus it is possible to describe the Teiger House in New Jersey as both rooted in and imposed upon its landscape. On the one hand, the L-shaped house fills a hole in the site, a shift between forest and field. The entrance drive follows an old bridle path, and the hickory forest's alternating light and shadow is echoed in both massing and detail. Stone lifted from the land itself was used for the entrance and the living room hearth. At certain times of day, those portions of the house clad in lead-coated copper simply "disappear" into the sky.

On the other hand, the architecture of this 6,400-square-foot house is generated not by nature but by geometry. The architects have imposed on the site an arbitrary ordering system based on a 40-foot square, which is broken down into 20-foot, 10-foot, and 4 by 5-foot modules. The smaller rhythms, set against the larger grids of 10 and 20, produce a kind of architectural syncopation akin to harmonics in music, with periodic points of resolution and congruence. This patterning is consistently applied at every level of architectural detail, such that the whole is present in each part, as it is in a DNA molecule.

The house is not situated at the brow of the hill but nestled into its gentle slope and entered at the bend in the L-shaped plan.

These geometries reach critical mass in the main living area, where all grids converge. At the same time, the "center" of the house is not static like the center of a circle, but moves with the visitor. If the language of the house is abstract, the experience is visceral.

In this regard, the Teiger House is a bridge project for principals Michael Rotondi and Clark Stevens. It serves as a transition between the more formal, geometric concerns of Morphosis, the firm Rotondi directed with Thom Mayne in the 1970s, and the interest in process, collaboration, and intuition that animates more recent projects by the now separate RoTo office. Among these projects is the new campus for the Sinte Gleska University of the Lakota Nation in Antelope, South Dakota. The Teiger House demonstrates RoTo's new emphasis on space and volume, not line, as the main determinants of architectural form.

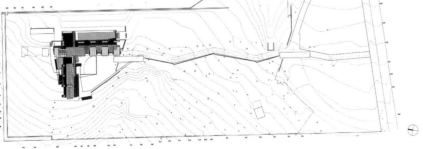

The house's organization is instantly visible from the air; on the ground, it is more gradually understood as visitors move into and through the building.

Just as Morphosis spoke to and for a generation of architects interested in the more cerebral side of their art, so the Teiger House is emblematic of several themes that dominate architectural discussions at the end of the twentieth century. The shaping of interior space that is simultaneously free-flowing and yet clearly demarcated for specific uses is a common preoccupation resolved in Teiger not by walls but by ceilings; the house section is manipulated to suggest what Rotondi calls limits without boundaries. The architects' desire to design a house that is at once multivalent, open, or indeterminate, and yet complete, is typical of their generation's desire to reconcile theory and practice.

Also visible in the stacked and shifted volumes of the Teiger House is an almost quixotic desire to imply motion in fundamentally static, built forms. The architects find a natural metaphor for both of these themes— indeterminacy and kinetics—in the currents of a river that are chaotic yet stable, ordered yet ever in motion. It is an image that speaks not only to the work of these particular architects but to the general dilemma of their profession, as it struggles with the paradox of building enduring works of art in an increasingly temporary world. ▪

The pool elevation is a dramatic composition of shifted or projecting planes and volumes.

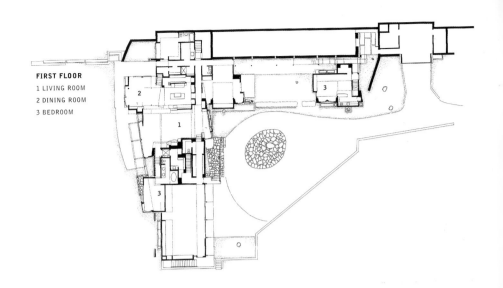

FIRST FLOOR
1 LIVING ROOM
2 DINING ROOM
3 BEDROOM

The main living spaces flow freely, their limits defined by structural elements and changes in ceiling height.

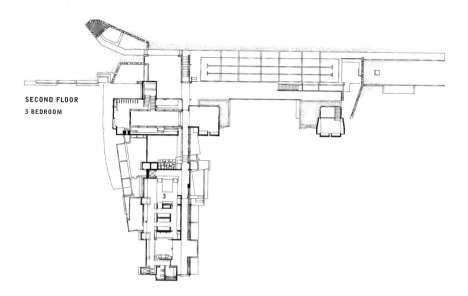

SECOND FLOOR
3 BEDROOM

3

The guest house is seen through an elegantly detailed brise soleil.

The front of the Croffead House, built of poured concrete and glass block, presents a firm silhouette against the sky. At the same time, the house defers to its natural context, being located on one corner of its site to maximize views of the waterways and to respect the ancient live oak trees.

CLARK & MENEFEE ARCHITECTS

CROFFEAD HOUSE CHARLESTON, SC

Cerebral yet earthy, dense and luminous, this modest-sized house sits confidently at the meeting of two waterways, making no effort to ingratiate itself to common tastes. The strength and elegance of its concrete and glass block front is undeniable, its squareness within the limpid landscape uncompromising, its modernity in the colonial heartland of the low country nothing short of brave. Like Stonehenge, it presents its stone-gray silhouette firmly against the horizon, strong yet enigmatic. It aligns itself with the forces of nature, its front wall angled to the main body of the house in response to an ancient row of live oak trees. And in contrast to the veiled message of its front, the house reveals to those who enter it an astonishing view of sky and landscape.

While it is thus moving in its own personal and site-inspired ways, the house owes a great debt to the work of two modern masters, the American Louis Kahn and the European Le Corbusier. Like Kahn, the architect W. G. Clark aimed for simple, modern monumentality through the large scale and solidity of the house's concrete front. This thick and massive zone communicates something of the building's structure and layout while providing a selective, filtered glimpse into and through the building with its use of glass block and clear glass. Clark, again emulating Kahn, separated the servant spaces—the exterior and interior stairs—from the served spaces, the internal body of the house. Also

The north side facade (above) has seventeen-foot-high industrial windows, offering dramatic views from the living room (opposite).

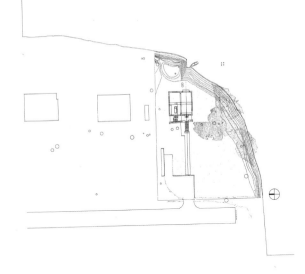

echoing Kahn's principles, the materials were chosen by the suitability of their properties: poured concrete is used for the front facade, which has large, sculptural openings; concrete block is used for the remaining facades, which have smaller windows; and all materials are resistant to the environmental problems of earthquake, salt air, and vermin.

At the same time, Clark, a professor at the University of Virginia, conceived of the main body of the house as a solution that can be generalized for a wide variety of problems, its free-flowing, interchangeable spaces reminiscent of the work of Le Corbusier. This main body, a simple cube, thirty-two feet on edge, with a central column, is divisible into eight smaller cubes (four quadrants on two levels), which can be combined or separated in almost infinite ways.

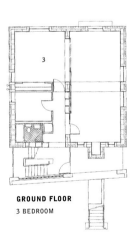

GROUND FLOOR
3 BEDROOM

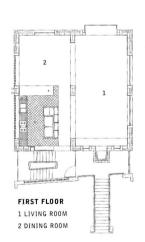

FIRST FLOOR
1 LIVING ROOM
2 DINING ROOM

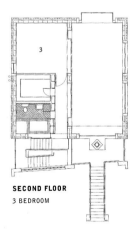

SECOND FLOOR
3 BEDROOM

The fireplace and chimney define the central axis of the nineteen-foot-high living room (opposite). A central pier, visible in the floor plan, divides the floors into quadrants. On the rear wall (above), a window loggia allows the living room to project almost into a stand of trees.

One of the possible permutations serves the current needs of the clients. Half of the eight cubes are combined into a brilliant two-story living room with seemingly endless views across the waterways. Two more cubes, one above the other, serve as dining space and master bedroom and open onto the living room. The remaining two cubes contain the most enclosed spaces—the kitchen on the main level, the bathrooms upstairs. These closed areas occupy one corner of the house, just as the house itself occupies one corner of the site and leaves the remaining space as open and free as possible. But in the future, for these or other occupants, any combination within the cube is possible. In addition, under the main cube of the house, a ground story contributes another set of quadrants, now used for a guest bedroom and the owner's art studio, but easily convertible into a new set of rooms.

In keeping with fundamental Modernist aspirations, the design, then, responds to both universal and specific conditions: it provides the framework for an almost infinite number of layouts, while bending for the trees and opening for the views of this individual site. ■

The glass block in the stairwell introduces light into the space. The stairwell is wedge-shaped in plan, since its front wall is angled to align with the row of live oak trees running through the site.

MOUNTAIN HOUSE **DILLARD, GA**

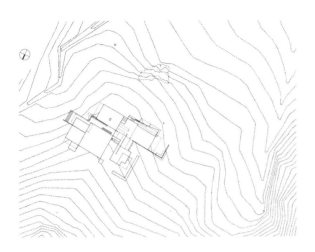

One of the threads running through the history of American architecture, and American Modernism in particular, is the relationship of building to landscape. The idea of blending in, of blurring the boundaries between inside and out, is identified in particular with Frank Lloyd Wright's Prairie houses. The opposite notion of defining a formal urban realm in the wilderness of nature informs Thomas Jefferson's University of Virginia campus.

Both models meet in the design of a 4,100-square-foot house in the Appalachian foothills by Atlanta architects Mac Scogin, Merrill Elam, and Lloyd Bray. The strategy of running long and low, working with the grain of the land, is clearly visible in the Wrightian plan of their Mountain House. All living spaces are organized on one floor, a move that will allow the clients eventually to use this weekend getaway as their primary residence in retirement.

The house is approached across a formal entry court built of stone from the site.

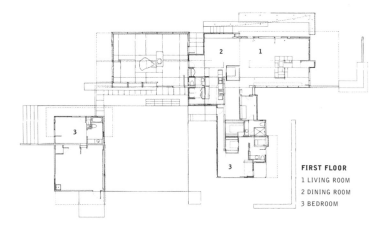

FIRST FLOOR
1 LIVING ROOM
2 DINING ROOM
3 BEDROOM

93

The unassuming front door (opposite) opens into a clerestory-lit gallery that leads to the living room.

94   The formal entrance court is intentionally urban in character, its raised surface laid with stones from the site, its edges defined by the guest house/garage, the master bedroom wing, and a large screened porch. The house itself grows increasingly informal as visitors move to and through it. They slip into the house at one corner of the court, entering a double-height gallery filled with the clients' collection of regional art. From this tall but constricted space, they pass into the wide open living room with its sweeping views down the hillside to a grassy pasture and mountains beyond. The transition from city to country is complete.

Concrete walls and wooden decks shape outdoor rooms that extend beyond the living room into the landscape. The house runs long and low in contrast to the surrounding birch trees (following pages).

The porch is anchored by a massive hearth. Steps behind the guest house can be used as a mini-amphitheater by a pond designed by the owner.

The living room finds its equal and opposite in the 900-square-foot screened porch, an outdoor room warmed like the rest of the house with subfloor radiant heating and therefore used year-round. These expansive, quasipublic spaces easily accommodate a crowd, yet little hideaways are scattered throughout, like the inglenook behind the living room fireplace; the study tucked aside the entrance gallery; and a little bay window in the master bath, which opens onto a private court enclosed by hemlocks.

These details and others, including the use of clerestory windows both to light the interior and to exaggerate the horizontal lines of the house, recall the work of Wright. Such affinities, however, are more in the line of family resemblances than they are direct quotations. Architects look at everything, says Merrill Elam—even basements. Impressed by the quality of concrete work in the basements of more conventional wood-frame houses in the area, which is one of the wettest in the United States, the architects chose to feature that material aesthetically. The house is raised on a concrete plinth as Wright himself might have done. Concrete walls cut through the house, extending beyond its perimeter to shape outdoor rooms that are at once part of and yet separate from the surrounding birch forest, as is the house itself. ■

DAN HOUSE
MALIBU, CA

Franklin D. Israel, who migrated to California from the East Coast, made art out of the ordinary, everyday architecture he found there. Unlike many of his peers whose work denies or combats the mass-market builder vernacular that surrounds them, Israel, who died in 1996, chose to regard that class of building as a legitimate source of inspiration. Like Frank Gehry, Israel was not identified with any particular school of thought; his work, however, is easily identified by its freewheeling exuberance, bold forms, and dramatic collages.

The Dan House started as a commission to expand a typical Malibu ranch house. One week before the clients were to move to rented accommodations for construction, the house burned to the ground. In its place, Israel and project architect Steven S. Shortridge proposed a long bar building that followed the footprint of the original ranch, as per building codes. The heart of the 5,100-square-foot house and the center of the bar is a combined living/dining/kitchen space; one end of the bar houses mirror-image children's bedrooms and the other end a three-car garage and maid's room. Appended to this long, vaulted volume on the street side is an angled entrance clad in shiny ZincAlum panels. On the opposite side of the bar, two free-form pavilions enjoy panoramic views of the canyon below and ocean beyond. One pavilion houses the master bedroom and studio above, the other a den, guest room, and office.

The entrance is clad in a folded grid of zinc aluminum panels. On the rear facade (following pages), the master bedroom and den/guest pavilions project from the long bar housing main living spaces.

This very clear articulation of parts, exaggerated on the house's exterior, is less dominant inside, where space and surfaces are handled more fluidly. Israel's fascination with folded planes is especially apparent in the living room, whose ceiling bends and folds to become the wall in a manner more reminiscent of origami than of conventional, 90-degree wall/ceiling junctures. Within this folding wrapper or skin, the skeleton or structure of the house is expressed in columns and beams. Free-flowing space is anchored by the chimney in the living room and by the spectacular pinwheel column and beams in the master bedroom.

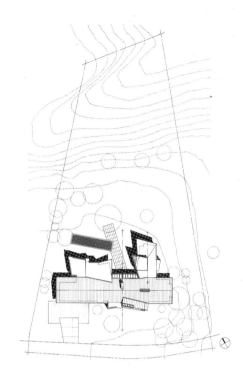

A skewed opening in the stucco wall reveals a second-floor study perched above the master bedroom (side view, above).

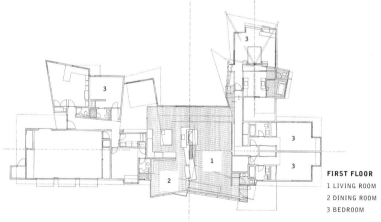

FIRST FLOOR
1 LIVING ROOM
2 DINING ROOM
3 BEDROOM

Douglas fir cabinets separate the dining room from the living room beyond.

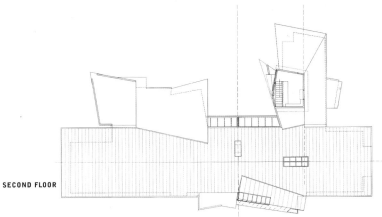

SECOND FLOOR

The dramatic master bedroom is designed as a poolside stageset.

This master bedroom is surprisingly monumental in character, rising up on the one hand toward the mountains and dipping down to ocean views on the other. It is also the house's most exuberant and sculptural piece, a dramatic counterpoint to the more severe bar to which it seems but lightly attached. A jazzy backdrop to the pool area, the wing evokes Israel's early work as a movie set designer in Hollywood.

The handling of the fenestration in the master bedroom, and other details such as the master bathroom wall, reveal the architects' debt to the work of Frank Lloyd Wright. The master bedroom's rear facade, on the other hand, is surfaced in banded stucco that recalls the unusually wide wood siding of the original ranch house. It is this combination of influences, both academic and vernacular, refined and ad hoc, that identifies Israel's work and anchors it in his adopted home, California. ■

A single, monumental column in the master bedroom supports a pinwheel of beams that fly up and out.

ANTOINE PREDOCK ARCHITECT

WHITE RESIDENCE PINNACLE PEAK, AZ

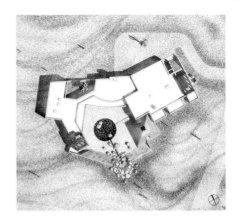

Albuquerque architect Antoine Predock is known as a "regionalist," having made his mark with buildings, such as the Nelson Fine Arts Center at Arizona State University and the Las Vegas Library, that celebrated and sanctified the Southwest. Although his work is by no means confined to that area, Predock's approach has been honed by the desert: its climatic exigencies, its fragile ecology, its danger, and its beauty. Anchored in the elements, his White Residence celebrates the desert triumvirate of earth, sun, and water in a building that is itself mountain and valley.

The 4,700-square-foot house is partially buried in the earth, a wise environmental choice, as it grants thermal stability to the spaces within. Bounded to the east by a sunrise pavilion and to the west by a sunset tower, the rooms in between follow the sun, from the east-facing breakfast nook through the main working and living spaces to the nocturnal bedroom wing.

111

The silhouette, punctuated by a sunset-viewing tower and mountain-shaped library, is analogous to the mountain range beyond.

Earth-toned stucco is applied to thick adobe walls that provide thermal stability.

FIRST FLOOR
1 LIVING ROOM
2 DINING ROOM
3 BEDROOM

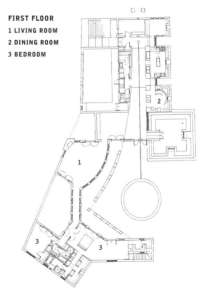

Predock believes architecture should engage all the senses, and here he uses water sparingly but to great effect, as a kind of auditory accompaniment to passage through the house. Noisy sprays of water mark the entrance; inside, a richer-sounding stream of water erupts from a black granite block and runs through a channel set in the hall floor to emerge outdoors, where it empties into a limpid pool. Another more naturalistic water course emerges from a cluster of boulders along the southern edge of the court. Sunlight, too, is manipulated for both aesthetic and pragmatic ends. A deep-set loggia protects the partially buried living room while affording views that skim across the surface of the desert. Trellises filter out the harshest rays, while courtyard stones collect heat that is released at night, when the desert cools down dramatically.

The house as a whole takes on the stern, archaic profile of a pueblo or Mayan ruin. In the face of the desert, says Predock, moldings and string courses seem fussy, superfluous. Predock's stark, simple forms appeal to fellow Modernists who seek a similarly timeless architecture; at the same time, his overtly metaphorical approach draws on a pre-Modern tradition in architecture. The end result may look intuitive or primitive, but it is very much the product of a late twentieth-century mind. ∎

Running water, the strong contrast of light and shade, and dramatic views of the desert—all are carefully choreographed to engage the five senses.

A water course accompanies passage through the house to the central court (following pages), which is viewed from the living room through a curving wall and deep loggia.

117

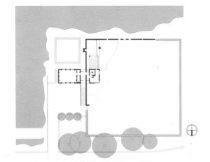

KNEE RESIDENCE NORTH CALDWELL, NJ

The Knee Residence demonstrates the latest in a series of studies of idealized house types developed by architects Laszlo Kiss and Tod Zwiegart, with Simon Ungers, over a fifteen- year period. The house also explores the intersection of two very different design paradigms—the Classical and the Modern.

The five-part series of house types has progressed as follows: a simple Platonic box, the Classical house prototype, in which the house is treated as an object in the landscape; the hollowed-out box, with the house as a donut with a courtyard at its center; the cross form, which is the inverse of the donut, with voids—courtyards—in four corners; the linear house, formed by squeezing the box until it is almost a wall; and the Modernist fragment, formed by squeezing the box in some other way, as realized in the Knee Residence.

The 4,000-square-foot Knee Residence was formed, in concept, by severing the perimeter of a square box at two opposite corners, and then squeezing together the two resultant L shapes until they interlocked. As seen in the floor plan, one of the L shapes is the house itself, and the other is a wall that extends into the landscape. The latter, a one-story concrete block wall, passes through the house, which is clad on its exterior in artificial stucco panels on aluminum channels. The wall divides the house into entry/family-room wing and living/dining/kitchen wing on the main floor. The mass that had been, in concept, at the center of the basic square box "oozed out" as the com- 121 pression occurred during the design of the house, and is expressed as the curved court-yard outside the living-room wing.

The second theme, the blend of Classical and Modern prototypes, is apparent throughout the house. The architects refer to the Classical type as "inscribed," because it is defined as a complete form, and the Modernist type as "implied," because of its fragmentary, incomplete nature. The contrast between these two types is apparent throughout the house, but can most easily be discerned from the courtyards formed by each of the major L shapes.

From the large, square courtyard defined by the L-shaped wall, the house itself is seen as a solid object—the Classical palazzo, the "inscribed" form—and the courtyard is a

An L-shaped wall of white concrete block slides beside the front door as it intersects with the stuccoed body of the house.

SECOND FLOOR
3 BEDROOM

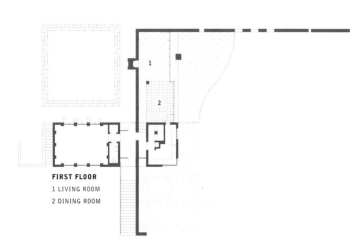

FIRST FLOOR
1 LIVING ROOM
2 DINING ROOM

The living/dining room is designed to be experienced as part of the exterior courtyard space beyond its glass walls. The L-shaped wall (following pages) defines a square courtyard outside the living room, separating the formal landscape from the natural wooded terrain beyond it.

complete square. In contrast, the living room itself, at the corner of this L shape, is an "implied" space: like a space by Modern master Mies van der Rohe, it is not complete in itself, but is part of the exterior courtyard space beyond its glass walls. To sum up: on this side of the house, the house and courtyard are "inscribed" and the interior space is "implied."

From the smaller, more private garden defined by the L of the house itself, the overall house is seen not as a complete, traditional object but as two walls, fragments remaining after the closed box was transformed. Similarly, the garden is defined only on these two sides: its nature, then, is fragmentary, or "implied." In contrast, the family room alongside this garden is a traditional, enclosed room; its Classical nature is underlined by architectural details, such as its set of three traditional French doors. Here, the house and courtyard are "implied" and the interior space is "inscribed."

The rich complexity of spaces resulting from these design ideas does not end at the perimeter of the house. The house and wall reach into the landscape—like in houses by Frank Lloyd Wright—and organize the one-acre site. In addition to the private rear garden behind the family room described above, a forecourt runs in front of the double garage beneath the family room, with a single dramatic flight of stairs leading along the block wall up to the entrance. Beside the living room is the large, classically square courtyard, also described above; and behind this square courtyard, reached through a set of three openings in the block wall (modern, frameless slots reinterpreting the three French doors of the family room), lies the natural wooded landscape, which harbors somewhere within it a naturalistic English garden. ∎

Outside the "implied" space of the living room (left), the courtyard and the house are complete, or "defined," forms. Outside the "defined" family room (above right), the garden and house are seen as "implied."

ERIC OWEN MOSS ARCHITECTS

Architecture is by nature geometric: it has dimension and volume that can be mathematically and geometrically ordered. A natural subtext in all architecture, geometry is the principal subject in some. The Lawson/Westen House, for example, was used by its architect Eric Owen Moss of Culver City, California, as a kind of laboratory in which he investigated the spatial and volumetric consequences of geometric manipulation. This interest in geometry, combined with an expressionistic handling of architectural form, is also typical of the larger commercial and institutional work that now dominates Moss's practice.

Programmatically, the 6,000-square-foot house revolves around the kitchen—center of daily life and entertainment in a family for whom cooking builds community. When they leave this common center, the kids migrate to one end of the house, the grown-ups to the other.

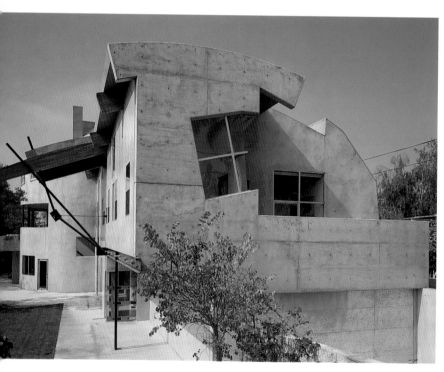

A beam projected over the entrance completes an ideal vault extending from the kitchen cylinder toward the street.

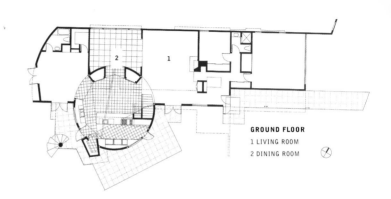

GROUND FLOOR
1 LIVING ROOM
2 DINING ROOM

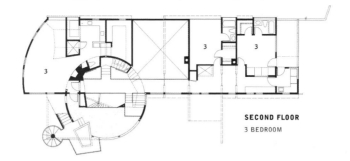

SECOND FLOOR
3 BEDROOM

Programmatic elements are the pretext for an exploration of form quite distinct from the idea of "house." And yet just as the kitchen is the heart of the home, so it is the center and starting point for a series of geometric moves that shape the principle spaces. The kitchen is a perfect cylinder, whose focal point in plan is the physical center of the site; its roof is a shifted cone. The cone top has been sliced vertically, producing a parabola, which, when extended toward the street, shapes a vaulted roof. The vault itself, however, is incomplete, the idealized form evident only at the entrance where an exposed beam locates its edge.

Moss exploits the tension produced between each new form and its antecedent: between cylinder and cone, cone and parabolic vault. This oscillation, swinging from forms we know and can name, toward the new, the complex, and the unrecognizable, is for Moss emblematic of life in the late twentieth century. Moreover, the house can only be understood through motion; there is no one fixed point at

131

The corner of the house is cut away to reveal a portion of the central cylinder, the starting point of the design.

132

which a visitor can say, "Aha! I get it now." Rather, perception is kinetic; each time you move, you must reassemble the picture. Nowhere is the importance of motion in the experience of space more evident than in the series of stairs and landings leading from the kitchen four flights up to the ocean view deck.

Other elements of the design challenge traditional norms in architecture. A window that scales the wall and climbs onto the roof asks the questions: What makes a window a window? What distinguishes wall from roof? Even the color of the exterior wall, which is covered in cement plaster that was applied with a steel trowel, is indeterminate, changing with light and position. It is, says Moss, no color you could name.

A catwalk above the living room passes through the stair tower, connecting front and rear bedrooms.

This fascination with indeterminacy in architecture links Moss up to a point with the so-called Deconstructivists. Equally, Moss's idiosyncratic, sculptural approach to architecture ties him to Frank Gehry, aesthetic mentor to so many California architects. Beyond these shared sensibilities, however, Moss's work is his own. Its willing awkwardness in the service of ideas and its muscular angularity have more in common with nineteenth-century Romantic Expressionism than with any particular twentieth-century paradigm. ∎

The stair tower is the dynamic heart of the house.

GROTTA HOUSE **HARDING TOWNSHIP, NJ**

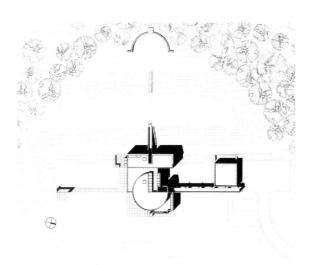

Richard Meier is one of the best-known living architects in the United States. He is the designer of the vast, high-profile Getty Center in Los Angeles, California. He was one of the first winners of the prestigious Pritzker Prize. He has designed buildings across America and in Europe that are always recognizable by the purity of their geometrical forms.

By now, the image of the Meier house is not unfamiliar. It comes easily to mind, the gleaming white sculpture of Platonic forms, on and through which light plays, sitting on the landscape. But it is absolutely riveting, indeed awe-inspiring, because it comes so very close to perfection in its own terms. Furthermore, it is one of the formative and representative architectural images for our times.

Meier strode into the world of architecture in the late 1960s, when he and several other young architects proposed a fundamental change in architectural direction. Rejecting

The central form of the gleaming white house is a cylinder. This cylinder, which contains the living room, is set into an orthogonal block. Radiating in three directions from the cylinder are walkways, one of which connects the house to a sculptural lookout in the site.

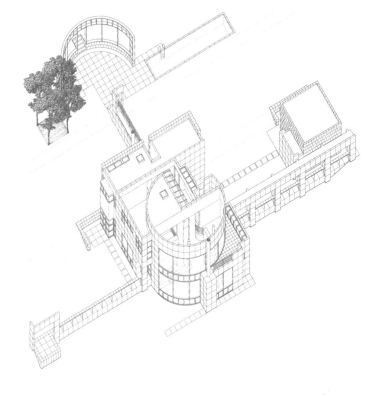

As seen in the drawing above, a colonnaded walkway connects the garage to the house, and a walkway/bridge (left in photo) connects the house to an open-air pavilion at the top of the site.

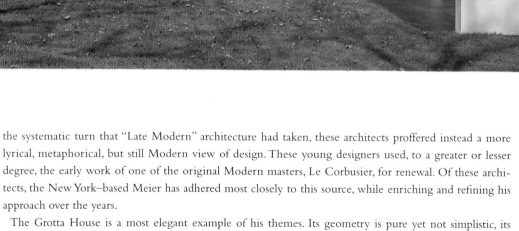

the systematic turn that "Late Modern" architecture had taken, these architects proffered instead a more lyrical, metaphorical, but still Modern view of design. These young designers used, to a greater or lesser degree, the early work of one of the original Modern masters, Le Corbusier, for renewal. Of these architects, the New York–based Meier has adhered most closely to this source, while enriching and refining his approach over the years.

The Grotta House is a most elegant example of his themes. Its geometry is pure yet not simplistic, its relationship with nature aristocratic but not unengaged. A two-story cylinder anchors the structure to its point on the site; three attenuated radial arms reach out in a perfect T-shape to three points on the compass, steadying the house's position and taking command of the gently sloping meadow.

This basic scheme is then further developed formally and spatially by rectilinear volumes that supplement and interrupt the cylinder, a form that, in fact, is never completed except in the mind's eye. Within the cylinder, the three established radii continue to serve as circulation paths both across and up through the house, while the fourth point of the compass is fixed by the fireplace chimney. Overlapping floor levels and a set of various but carefully orchestrated windows and skylights add to the stimulating complexity of the house. As is usual in a Richard Meier house, the spatial excitement is set off by a very simple

The simple geometric elegance of the living room (opposite and above) sets off the clients' collection of craft objects. The master bedroom (above top) is located on the second-floor balcony overlooking the living room.

The walkway leading from the garage to the house is covered and lined with columns on one side, rectangular piers on the other. While the house itself is clad in porcelain-enameled steel panels, the garage walls are made of ground-faced concrete block.

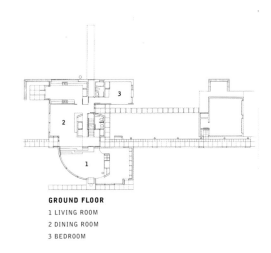

GROUND FLOOR
1 LIVING ROOM
2 DINING ROOM
3 BEDROOM

146

palette of materials: white porcelain-enameled steel panels, ground-faced concrete block, and stucco on the exterior; and white-painted wallboard, with slate and oak flooring, on the inside.

Meier houses are not easy to live up to, given their perfectionism. In some, environmental considerations, notably daylight control, have been compromised in the interest of uncompromised art. But their residents almost always find it worthwhile to adapt, and always find them stimulating.

In the Grotta House, the perfect white background provides, interestingly enough, the ideal foil for a collection of wood and textile craft objects. It is symptomatic of Meier's magic that in both the Grotta and the Hoffman (page 184) Houses, otherwise undramatic sites are transformed into ideal canvases. In Meier's hands, plainness becomes sublime simplicity. ▪

Radial axes form part of the precise geometry of the house and are defined by a number of elements, including the walkways, the chimney, and the skylit central stairway.

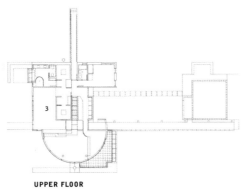

UPPER FLOOR

3 BEDROOM

MORPHOSIS

Some architects can't wait to get beyond single-family house commissions; others, however, return again and again to this most elemental of building types, and the evolution of their theory and practice can be read in successive house designs. Morphosis of Los Angeles belongs to the latter camp. The architects have designed other larger works such as the Cedars-Sinai Cancer Center in Los Angeles, designed by Morphosis principal Thom Mayne with former partner Michael Rotondi. Their houses, however, present an unusually coherent series, each one evolving out of its predecessor. The Blades Residence, shown here, moves beyond design ideas explored in the previous and well-published Crawford Residence. At the same time, the specificities of client, site, community planning regulations, and materials make the Blades house a unique work of art.

148

A brush fire in 1990 destroyed the clients' original residence, leaving the architects with a virtual tabula rasa. (The same could be said of the client, a sculptor whose entire collection was eliminated and whose work has since taken a new direction.) An empty site allowed the architects complete freedom to explore long-standing preoccupations, principally the balance between typology, or the underlying order of architecture, and idiosyncratic "events."

The front entrance is recessed in the redwood street wall, while a concrete ellipse (visible at right) curves out to enclose a private precinct (following pages).

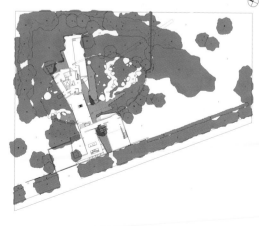

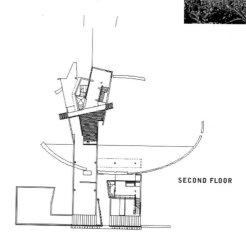

The Blades house is characteristically self-referential, turning away from the surrounding one-acre zoned, rural-suburban context to create an inner world. Space or volume in the 4,500-square-foot house is not the first focus of architectural invention but rather the outcome of decisions made primarily in plan. A cast-concrete wall, elliptical in plan, is imposed on the site, creating a perfect, Platonic form against which all other architectural decisions play. Once the ellipse was drawn on the site, it provided a boundary between outside and in. The house's more public spaces—the entrance and main living/entertaining space, a studio/gallery accessible to the public, and the garage—were placed outside the ellipse in an elongated bar. The more private rear wing of the house runs perpendicular to this bar within the sheltering elliptical curve; here rooms are arranged sequentially, culminating in the master bedroom suite, which noses into the earth.

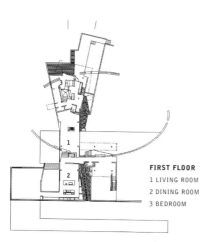

FIRST FLOOR

1 LIVING ROOM

2 DINING ROOM

3 BEDROOM

SECOND FLOOR

A study above the master bedroom projects out over the pool. Beside it, the massive, vaulted metal roof touches down.

An elaborate system of pulleys and weights controls the fireplace; beyond it lies the master bedroom suite, with its studio above overlooking the pool.

The progression from public to private space is paralleled by a development from the more controlled, straightforward front bar to the increasingly random and complex rear wing. A grid of columns is first established and then ignored; walls splay; the studio above the master bedroom seems to take off in flight. At the same time, a vaulted metal roof ties the whole together.

This idea of developing a system that is then "violated" is emblematic of an architecture that is its own subject, object, and verb, a system in which luxury is conveyed not by the use of expensive materials but through the complexity of architectural form and the elaboration of structural elements. The Blades Residence is quintessential Morphosis: complex, cerebral, fascinating. ∎

The elliptical wall cuts through the living room (opposite) and the master bedroom (above). The client himself took a blow torch to the concrete form work, producing an unusual, flamed finish.

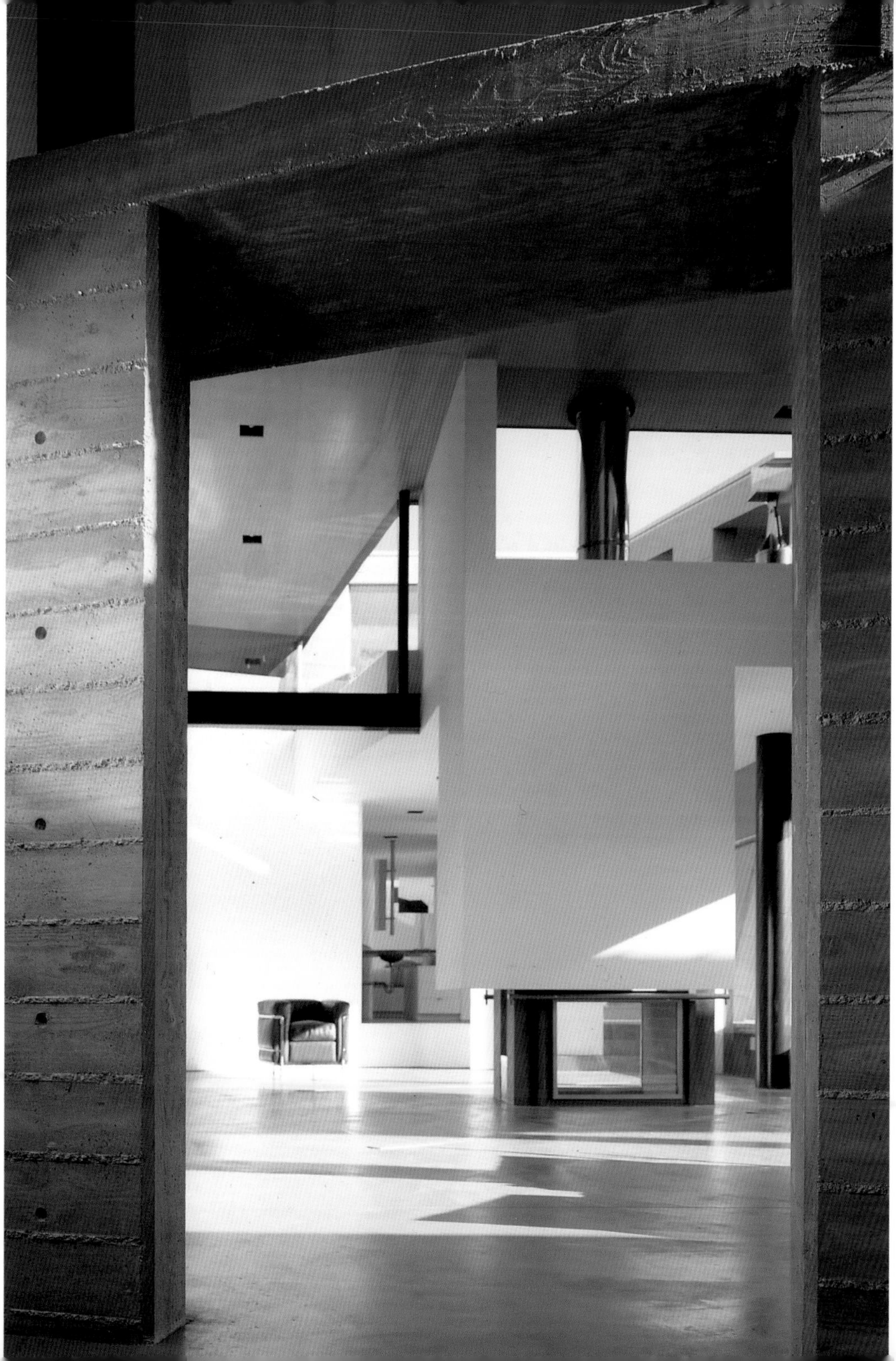

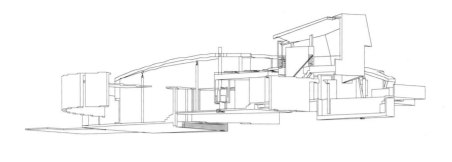

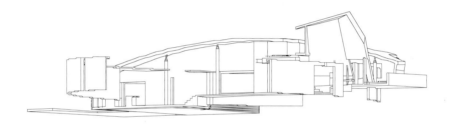

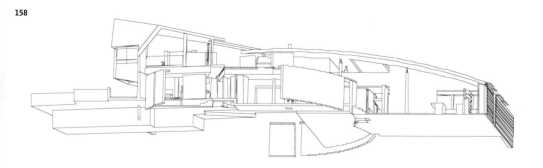

The intersection of structural elements is meticulously detailed and provides the house's only ornamentation.

MACHADO AND SILVETTI ASSOCIATES

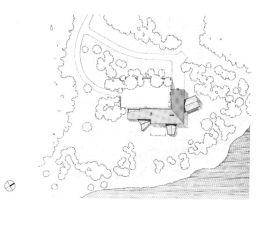

The work of Rodolfo Machado and Jorge Silvetti serves as a bridge in two senses. The designs are stimulating both intellectually and sensually, connecting theory and practice. And they form a bridge as well between Postmodernism and Modernism, combining elements from a variety of traditions but filtering them through an abstract lens.

The Concord House by these two Argentinian-born, Boston-based architects, for example, is a montage of numerous building types. While the assembly of traditional building forms is reminiscent of 1980s Postmodernism, in this case both the forms and the overall composition are abstracted. At the same time, materials on two of the facades are quite different from materials on the other facades; while the juxtaposition is heterogeneous in concept, it is orderly and architectural in execution.

161

The main volume of the house is L shaped, partially enclosing a rectangular entrance courtyard. The outer walls of this volume take advantage of fine views over the wooded site and toward a large private pond. Attached to the outer perimeter of this main volume are three ancillary volumes, serving as living room, breakfast room, and screened porch, respectively.

The exterior perimeter of the L-shaped house is sheathed in white clapboard and punctured by "special" volumes. The volume of the screened porch expands outward and upward; the breakfast room volume tapers as it projects outward.

The slate and cedar walls of the courtyard suggest remains of local barns. Aligned with the entrance to the courtyard is a pointed window niche (opposite top) in the library.

If we examine this 12,000-square-foot house starting at its entrance, we begin first with the wall lining two sides of the entrance court, that is, the inner walls of the main volume. These walls—consisting of a slate base and "rusticated" natural cedar siding with deep battens—function as fictitious "existing" barn walls about which the new house is built (as, in truth, has happened in many structures in the area).

As we move into the principal volume, we find a rhythmic layout of rooms: main room/ service room/main room/service room and so on, with windows responding to that

alternating pattern. The outer perimeter of the volume is clad in white-painted cedar siding with divided light windows, intentionally reminiscent of New England Colonial architecture. Without an expressed roof, however (the single pitch of the roof slopes toward the courtyard), without rosettes, and with minimal trim, the house from this side evokes a Shaker aesthetic. Although the Shakers never settled in Concord, the simplified language is appropriate in the context of the unadorned elegance of the local architecture.

The ancillary volumes attached to the main volume enrich the formal language of the house and vary the visual axes dramatically. The first element is the living room, angled so that it creates a richness of vistas from the front door. Since the room's use is formal, a kind of Classical language was chosen, with traditional elements such as French doors and coffered ceiling. Once again, however, the chosen language is simplified, and its elements—its fireplace, the staircase screen wall and railing, and the ceiling—read as mid-century Modern pieces.

The living room (opposite) is the most formal of the special volumes.
The stairway divides the living room from the entrance hall (above).

The second attached volume is the breakfast room. Like the living room, it manipulates the view. In this case, the room tapers as it projects perpendicular to the kitchen, creating an elongated perspective toward the pond. Less formal than the living room, the breakfast room expresses its post-and-beam construction. At the same time, with its white paint and divided light windows, the room has a familiar, cozy, bourgeois suburban feel.

The screened porch, employing unpainted post-and-beam construction, is the most earthy and yet the most abstractly Modernist of the house's ancillary elements. Like the living room, it meets the main volume in an acute angle and "deforms" that volume; like the breakfast room, it is angled, but in this case expansively, almost explosively, with its upturned butterfly roof. It seems to imply not only the future swimming pool on its axis but the whole sweep of the landscape. It could be a metaphor for the overall house: regular in shape and kaleidoscopic in view. ■

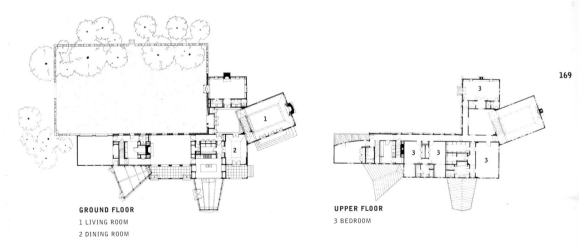

GROUND FLOOR

1 LIVING ROOM

2 DINING ROOM

UPPER FLOOR

3 BEDROOM

The breakfast room (above) tapers toward the outside, while the screened porch (opposite) expands.

KONING EIZENBERG ARCHITECTURE

The renovation and expansion of a suburban Spanish bungalow has given the house new presence and architectural character.

One of many paradoxes that characterize the history of Modern architecture is the evolution of two diametrically opposite points of view about the role of the architect. On the one hand are the "heroic" Modernists—independent, dedicated above all to the art of architecture, client be damned—and on the other, the architect as servant functionalist, a self-effacing space manager. Most architects would locate themselves on the continuum between these two extremes, or, as architect Julie Eizenberg puts it succinctly, somewhere between a prima donna and a doormat.

It is in fact possible to argue that, far from developing a set style in the manner of hero architects, Eizenberg and partner Hank Koning change their approach, or their position along that continuum, from project to project. Originally from Australia, the pair are at home in eclectic California. Their institutional work, which includes several award-winning social housing projects, shows a certain consistency of style and method. Their single-family houses, however, are extremely varied, as the two included in this volume demonstrate (see also page 176). This work eludes classification, a fact that may well please these architects, who enjoy the emigré's freedom both to criticize and to appropriate elements of the culture in which they find themselves.

Eizenberg believes the general public has never recovered from the assault of Modern architecture; thus to be a Modernist or even a "soft Modernist," as she describes the approach their firm takes, requires first establishing trust between architect and client. This relationship is particularly apparent in the house on 31st Street in Santa Monica, a low-budget project undertaken by clients who weren't at all sure that they needed Architecture with a capital A. This renovation/expansion of a typical Spanish Mediterranean bungalow is not at all about "object-making," the focus of heroic Modernism, but about space and sequence, accommodation and relationship. The 650-square-foot addition echoes and elevates the language of the original 1,300-square-foot house in a manner deliberately reminiscent of the work of Irving Gill, one of California's original soft Modernists. Scale, spatial progression, and views are carefully manipulated to control how the house is experienced and even how large it feels. The design contrives to disappear, and the hand of the architects is hard to find without a direct comparison of before and after.

The design creates a variety of outdoor experiences, from a walled courtyard open to the sky, to an outdoor room that is covered but open on three sides, to the garden itself.

White stucco walls and openings punched through them produce wonderfully deep shadows and cool spaces. These details, which appear to be drawn from regional or vernacular traditions, are handled in a distinctly Modernist manner. Ornament or decoration is restricted to light, shadow, and landscape. The line between outdoors and in, a common Modernist preoccupation, is deliberately blurred in a sequence that moves from the kitchen/dining area to an outdoor patio open to the sky, to a covered outdoor room open to the elements on three sides, and finally to the garden.

This sequence, with its attendant changes in view and scale, is designed to be felt, not photographed; people provide the interest and scale in a design that is more suggestion than statement. ▪

SECOND FLOOR
3 BEDROOM

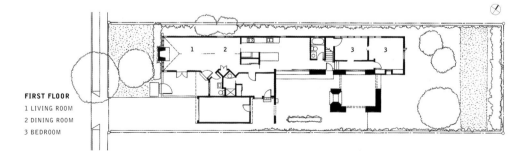

FIRST FLOOR
1 LIVING ROOM
2 DINING ROOM
3 BEDROOM

Ornament or decoration in the house is described through the subtle manipulation of light and shadow.

Designed by Hank Koning and Julie Eizenberg in collaboration with the late landscape architect Robert Fletcher, the Tarzana House is more about landscape than about architecture. A modest budget favored trees over expensive materials for the 3,000-square-foot residence, which is set in a rustic San Fernando Valley subdivision named for the famous jungle man created by a one-time resident.

The house itself is treated as a transition between one distinct type of outdoor space and another. The motor court and the entry court are hot, dry, winter spaces; the rear garden is a cool, green summer's paradise of unmowed grass and crape myrtles. Early sketches of the house, drawn in the loose style of Le Corbusier, make no distinction at all between outdoors and in. The living room, whose undulating roof also echoes Le Corbusier, is treated as an extension of the garden, not the other way around. The most enclosed and sheltered space in the house is the entry court, whose bright yellow walls recall the color-saturated architecture of Mexican architect Luis Barragan.

177

From the motor court (right), the house is entered through a bright, warm "winter" court.

The stair, with its horizontal metal mullions, is a classic Modern piece, while the color-saturated courtyard walls evoke the work of Luis Barragan. The garden facade (following pages) draws on Case Study Houses.

SECOND FLOOR
3 BEDROOM

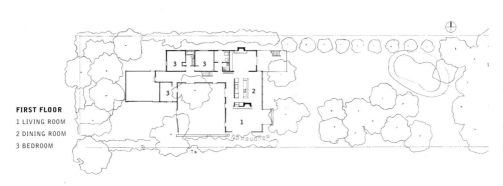

FIRST FLOOR
1 LIVING ROOM
2 DINING ROOM
3 BEDROOM

The house itself, however, owes less to Barragan than to Charles Eames, Craig Elwood, and other architects of the so-called Case Study Houses of the late 1940s and early '50s. The living room's rear elevation, a grid of glass whose bottom edge floats just above the ground, is clearly drawn from this Modernist tradition. Other details, including the wood sheathing and horizontal metal mullions, recall the peculiarly American—and more specifically Californian—Modernism of that era. The house has an almost "retro" feel, which continues in the handling of cabinetry and furnishings.

Although stylistically unrelated to Koning Eizenberg's 31st Street House in Santa Monica (page 170), Tarzana betrays similar preoccupations with sequence and movement through space, and with the treatment of landscape as an extension of architecture or vice versa. Drawn from different chapters of American Modernism, the houses together allude to the rich variety implicit in a style often maligned for its narrowness of vision. ▪

Living and dining spaces are treated as extensions of the garden, which is itself treated as an outdoor room.

STAMBERG AFERIAT ARCHITECTURE

How do you make an addition to a building that, in design terms, is a closed and complete form? And how do you approach such a task when the building—an early house designed by the now-renowned architect Richard Meier—has become legendary?

Generally, architects consider two broad strategies for adding to a structure: their design either contrasts with the existing building or continues its vocabulary. Since Peter Stamberg and former Meier employee Paul Aferiat share Meier's design sensibilities, it was natural that they would choose the latter approach in expanding his 1967 Hoffman House: in the addition, as in the original house, simple geometric forms would be rendered in nearly seamless white materials (see Grotta House, page 136). But they also understood that the original design was complete on its own terms. On a flat, almost square site, Meier had developed a self-fulfilled object, a volume of two overlapping rectangles, one parallel to the site and one diagonal to it. If they were going to keep the vocabulary, Stamberg and Aferiat knew they had to change the compositional strategy.

Expanding the 2,000-square-foot house to accommodate visiting grandchildren, the young New York architects (who were recommended for the job by Meier himself) took cues from the almost unfenestrated entrance wall. Instead of viewing this wall as merely one part of the building's envelope, they saw that it could be understood as a planar element in its own right and be extended into the landscape beyond the original sculptural form. The wall-as-landscape-element is a concept emphasized by Frank Lloyd Wright and used by Meier in more recent houses. This idea permitted the architects to see the rotated rectangles as objects

On the entrance side of the house, the addition (left in photo), like the original house, is unfenestrated. On the garden side of the house (overleaf) the large glazed volume accommodates the extended living room and follows the form of the original terrace.

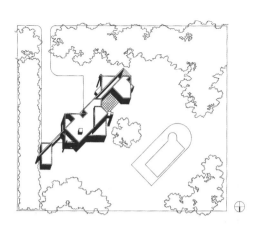

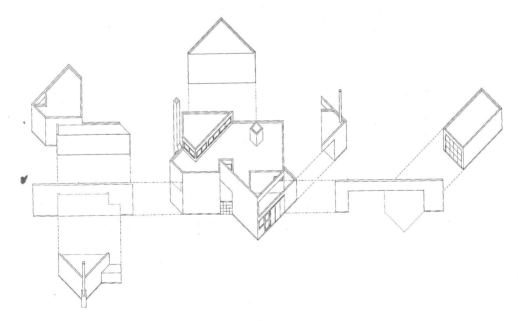

The original house as designed by Richard Meier, from the entrance side (above top) and the garden side (opposite). The drawing above shows the original house at the center and the additions on three sides. The garage at the right of the drawing has not yet been built.

playing off not only the ground plane but the wall plane as well. In design terms, this approach "allowed" them to create a second similar volume, also playing off the wall plane, for the extension.

This second volume, twenty-two by forty-four feet like the original house but only one story high, encompasses the master bedroom suite and a large recessed terrace. In turn, the original structure was rendered more commodious by enclosing the original terrace to enlarge the living room, reworking some of the existing rooms to accommodate more kitchen space, and combining upstairs spaces in order to convert bed niches into more generous bedrooms. Coincidentally, the extension of the solid wall into the landscape added a psychological and physical barrier between public and private domain, much needed by people who live in legends.

The now-ample living room follows Meier's established theme of overlapping volumes. The second-floor corridor (opposite top) overlooks the main space below.

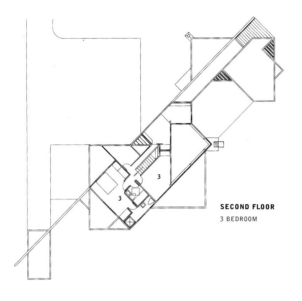

SECOND FLOOR
3 BEDROOM

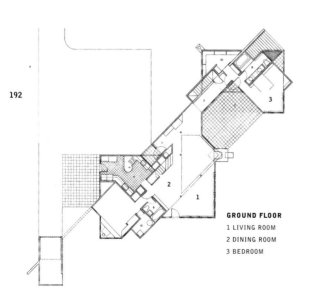

GROUND FLOOR
1 LIVING ROOM
2 DINING ROOM
3 BEDROOM

Inevitably, some of the clarity of the original design is lost in this more complicated scheme. But the new design demonstrates remarkable intellectual agility: the ability to convert the sculpture-on-the-ground-plane into two sculptures against two intersecting planes, all the while remaining faithful to the original vocabulary. As to the details, all are inspired by the original house, with technological improvements. Exterior walls have been stuccoed in keeping with the abstraction of the design; deteriorated painted wood windows have been replaced with white aluminum-wrapped ones; and air conditioning has been introduced. Mrs. Hoffman, who always loved the aesthetics of the original house, now finds material comfort, as well, in her enlarged space. ■

The large cube of the living room and smaller cube of the master bedroom both face the swimming pool.

SEADRIFT LAGOON HOUSE STINSON BEACH, CA

Born and educated in South Africa, Stanley Saitowitz is a first-generation California architect who works in San Francisco. His house on Seadrift Lagoon, designed for Jim and Mary Lou McDonald, is typical of his work—both modern and metaphorical. At 1,200 square feet, the house is neither large nor lavish: an exercise in minimalism. At the same time, this small house takes on a pair of related meta-phors. It is a boat, adrift on an ocean that can be heard from its deck but not seen. It is also a shell, protecting inhabitants from the cold-beach climate of northern California.

Saitowitz calls the design an exercise in form and space, not in materials. Simple particleboard, drywall, and vinyl flooring shape a combination kitchen/living/dining space that also answered the clients' desire for a complete contrast to their Victorian home in nearby San Francisco. Paired bedrooms and baths open, like the living room, onto a wooden deck overlooking Seadrift Lagoon.

The house turns an elegant, curved back to the harsh winds of northern California.

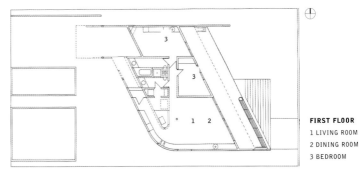

These living spaces are sheltered from northwest winds by a curving redwood-clad wall that extends beyond the corner of the living room to protect the deck. Small windows cut into this shell offer glimpses of nearby mountains and water. The roof lifts to admit reflections from the lagoon that play on the ceiling. The use of redwood siding, which has been detailed like lap siding on a ship, the deck's sharp prow, and even the sail-shaped window in the living room reinforce the sense of connection to and yet protection from the elements, which is the essence of a sea voyage.

The roof lifts dramatically at the corner to let in light.

Although the land around Seadrift Lagoon has been sub-divided over the last ten years and built up with a variety of ordinary suburban house types, several of the original clapboard beach houses remain in the area, and it is their relaxed simplicity, their almost rustic feel, that Saitowitz sought to emulate. Generations of architects have been in-spired by California vernacular; William Wurster and Ber-nard Maybeck, for example, looked to traditional handbuilt wooden buildings for inspiration. Saitowitz approaches these models from a Modernist's perspective, connecting at the level of expression, or "feel," and not detail. ∎

The deck is shaped like the prow of a ship; a bedroom window is a whimsical porthole.

CASA **LOS ANDES**
LIMA, PERU

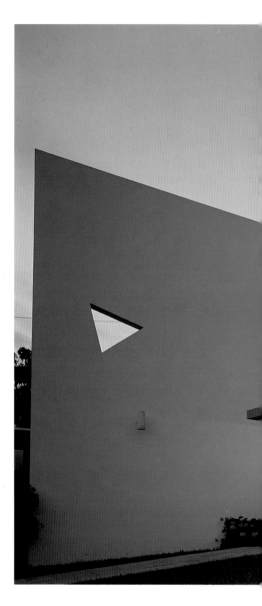

The Miami firm of Arquitectonica—Laurinda Spear and Peruvian-born Bernardo Fort-Brescia—were the *wunderkinder* of the late 1970s and '80s, having established themselves in critical circles and in the world of big building while still in their late twenties. Their own particular brand of Modernism, which combined intuition and rational thinking, glamour and technical slickness, childlike colors and adult fantasies, and individualistic design sense and a knowledge of big business, became evident in large-scale Miami apartment projects like the Atlantis and the Palace, simultaneously pleasing developers and exciting their peers. Their success continues to this day, with science museums, arenas, schools, office buildings, and hotels designed for sites across the country and in Europe.

The architects were always able to distance themselves from their architectural forms as they designed them, so that they could see them as both smaller-than-life—as intersecting toylike pieces highlighted with bright color—and as larger-than-life—as a series of vignettes representing a glamourized view of real life. As such, they represent both childlike innocence and a high degree of sophistication. This 3,500-square-foot house, built on a rectangular lot in a fashionable neighborhood in Lima, reflects their approach.

The piano-shaped entrance hall is framed by two extended planar walls; both the windows and wall cutouts underline a theme of randomness.

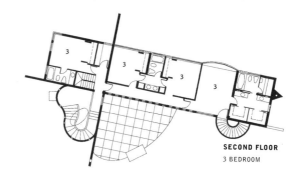

SECOND FLOOR

3 BEDROOM

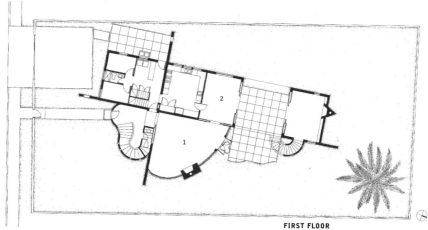

FIRST FLOOR

1 LIVING ROOM

2 DINING ROOM

Randomly placed windows and skylight heighten the entrance hall's drama (opposite).

The architects explain that the original design proposal featured four different towers "floating" in a pool that was to fill the whole site. The clients, however, decided against the pool. Instead, the architects "floated" the house within the grassy lot, the towers becoming four quadrants divided by two intersecting planes. The planes lie at an angle to the high walls around the lot, as if adrift in the green lawn. Tied in to the theme of floating is a theme of randomness, especially evident in the variety and placement of the windows.

The living room's curved glass wall seems almost to disappear, especially when seen against the strong chimney and door frame.

The volumes within the quadrants were each designed to be special in form. Freest of all is the voluptuous piano-shaped, pink entrance hall, pierced with randomly placed square windows as well as a round window and an elliptical skylight. The living room, too, is sensuous in shape. Its exterior wall, a segment of an oval, is made of frameless glass, allowing the division between inside and garden almost to dissolve visually. Setting off these two curvilinear volumes is a rectangular bar containing the more private rooms.

Still, there was more to come. Colored elements were added to the basic volumes, like pieces of modernist jewelry on an already stunning outfit. There is a red entrance canopy, red fireplaces, and a yellow spiral staircase connecting the library to the master bedroom.

Finally, there was the refinement of the facades. Each facade was laid out to "look nice," say the architects, two-dimensionally. In addition to the interesting variety of windows—those little square entrance hall ones, the glazed corners of the guest bedrooms reminiscent of early Modern architecture, and the limpid curved living room glazing—there are various cutouts on the main axial walls, which extend beyond the volumes. These openings serve to emphasize the walls' abstract, planar nature.

Described by its architects, the design seems to be the result of step-by-step pragmatic decisions. Is it simple? Not at all. Rather, it is a highly accomplished version of glamour and sophistication, American style. ∎

The red-framed opening in the street wall is a terse indication of the voluptuous architecture within.

STEVEN HOLL ARCHITECTS

BERKOWITZ-ODGIS HOUSE
MARTHA'S VINEYARD, MA

In Steven Holl's hands, not only is architecture "frozen music" (as the common metaphor goes); it can be "frozen literature," "frozen science," and so on, depending on the circumstances. In other words, it reaches beyond the confines of architectural types and into other disciplines suggested by the specific architectural commission.

By the late 1980s, after ten years as a practitioner in New York and a professor at Columbia University, Holl realized that architecture referring only to itself had a dead-end quality, and he began experimenting with ideas from other disciplines in order to stimulate the design process. The first building to benefit from this approach was the Berkowitz-Odgis house.

Until this 2,800-square-foot vacation house, Holl's design had been exemplary for its reductivist, Rationalist quality: the unornamented wall spoke of the essence of wallness; the windows were barely more than the necessary openings; a pyramidal skylight might represent a stark roof. The "essential house" would be refined only by subtle color, texture, detailing, and proportioning.

A wooden structure forms a porch outside the house's main body, and expresses the idea of "skeleton." The notion was inspired by Indian structures described in Herman Melville's Moby Dick.

With the Berkowitz–Odgis House, Holl took reductivist architecture as a foundation and developed it further by applying a system of metaphors from literature. He turned to Herman Melville's *Moby Dick* and was inspired by Melville's description of an unusual dwelling type made by Indians on Martha's Vineyard and Nantucket. They pulled the skeletons of beached whales onto dry land and transformed them into houses by stretching skins or bark over them.

Moved by the vision of the looming frame of bones, Holl took the skeleton of the American wood house—the balloon frame—and exposed it. Holl placed the walls within the frame instead of over it, creating a set of verandas facing the views. The house, set well up onto dry land because of building code requirements, became a permanent "beached whale" skeleton. Built of natural wood, also dictated by code, the frame soon weathered to an ashen gray.

Within the skeletal frame, the rooms are arranged as a row of elements perpendicular to the view. The plan gently cascades from the second-level master bedroom at the rear, which commands ocean views and benefits from access to a roof deck, down to the living room at the front. Volumetrically, the outstanding elements are the kitchen/dining room with triangular structures in plan and section, and the master bedroom tower.

The prow-shaped dining area (opposite and above) protrudes through the wood porch frame, which incorporates a diagonally patterned railing.

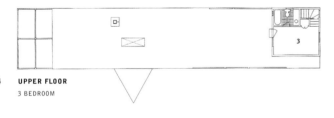

To the casual viewer, this is just a long, somewhat unusual wood house with verandas. But it has a number of meanings. With its exposed six-by-six-inch wood frame, it reads as a demonstration of the construction process. With its linear form and broad decks overlooking the Vineyard Sound, it evokes the shape of a ship. With its weatherbeaten finish, it refers to the interaction of manmade structures and harsh nature. With its austerity, it implies primitive shelter. To the architect, who by his very profession is a great observer and integrator of forms and maker of connections, all these and more undoubtedly apply. What, then, is the importance of the specific Melville metaphor? It offered an inspirational frame upon which to develop a poetic piece of architecture linked to the site. ■

214 **UPPER FLOOR**
3 BEDROOM

FIRST FLOOR
1 LIVING ROOM
2 DINING ROOM
3 BEDROOM

The freestanding chimney, finished in rough stucco, serves the living room fireplace (opposite) and the kitchen stove ventilation hood (above).

STEVEN HOLL ARCHITECTS

MAKUHARI HOUSING CHIBA, JAPAN

The Makuhari Housing development takes strides toward mending the unfortunate divide between two closely related programs, that of the private house and of multiple-unit housing. For the 190-unit complex in Japan, American architect Steven Holl incorporates individual houses into an otherwise repetitive unit scheme. This strategy tends to humanize and alter the focus of the large project, as does another Holl tactic—the transformation of a literary vision into architectural terms.

The core program for a multiple-unit housing project is much the same as that for an individual house—a place where people can retreat daily from the greater world, live privately, and, ideally, emerge nurtured and refreshed. But the design of the two types has diverged. The zeal of the early European modernists to achieve a housing utopia went too far in this country after World War II: architects, finding individual house design scarcely worthy of attention, focused ultimately futilely upon social engineering; at the same time, unrealistic hopes were placed in building technology to cut building costs through innovation. Saddled with too many expectations and too few successes, however, multiple housing had by the 1970s acquired the image of the poor relative, architecturally speaking, compared to the individual house.

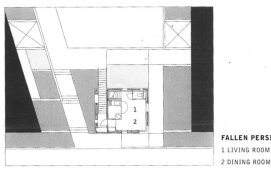

FALLEN PERSIMMON HOUSE
1 LIVING ROOM
2 DINING ROOM

The Fallen Persimmon House, a duplex apartment clad in zinc, stands at the west gate entrance to the Makuhari Housing complex.

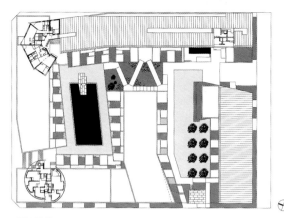

SITE PLAN

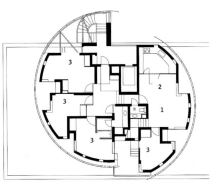

COLOR REFLECTING HOUSE

1 LIVING ROOM
2 DINING ROOM
3 BEDROOM

The Color Reflecting House is a circular penthouse apartment on the roof of one of the "heavyweight" apartment buildings. The heavyweight buildings (opposite) wrap around and into the one-block site, creating two semi-public gardens within the site.

WATER REFLECTING HOUSE
2 DINING ROOM

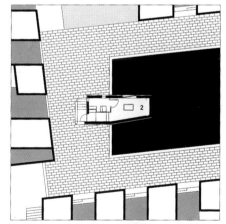

Steven Holl has attempted to change this dreary image. When he designed a mixed-use building in Seaside, Florida, he spiced up the repetitive apartments by adding a set of individualistic units responding to the "personalities" of imaginary artist occupants. In the Makuhari Housing project shown here, he sought to humanize the design by conceiving a set of gardens and six special houses that would create a sense of place. Holl based the design on *The Narrow Road to the Deep North*, which relates the inner journey of its author, the Japanese poet Basho.

Holl began the design by conceiving two semipublic gardens for the interior of the block, formal interpretations of his readings from Basho, which would serve as vestibules to the residential buildings. Around the gardens, he arranged five five-story rectangular buildings made of concrete,

The Water Reflecting House, which cantilevers over a pool in the north semipublic garden, serves as a communal tearoom.

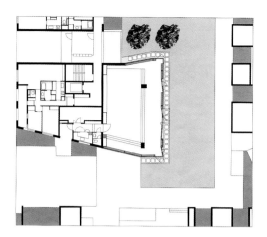

HOUSE OF THE BLUE SHADOW

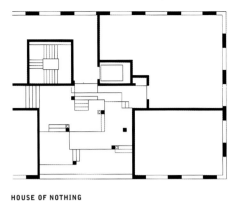

HOUSE OF NOTHING

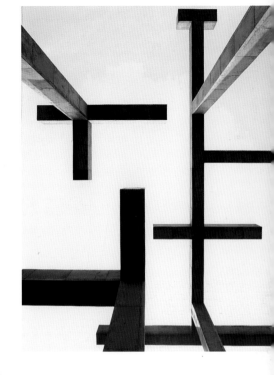

which he calls "silent" or "heavyweight" structures because they bracket the site and contain the majority of the dwelling units. These fairly regular buildings bend in unusual ways, both to create view corridors and to respond to the Japanese building code requirement for four hours of sunlight daily per apartment.

The views into the gardens from the street are carefully composed with the help of the six special metal-clad houses, called "activist" or "lightweight" structures, based on the Basho work. In contrast to the "silence" of the heavyweight structures, these activist structures are thought of as "sound"-producing. Two of the activist houses—the Sunlight Reflecting House and the Color Reflecting House, both penthouse structures on heavyweight buildings—are market-rate, individually owned apartments, as are about 75 percent of the units in the complex. Like the remaining units, the zinc-clad towerlike Fallen Persimmon House is a subsidized rental unit. The other three activist houses are communal spaces: the Water Reflecting House is a tearoom for meditation and small meetings; the House of the Blue Shadow, a large meeting room for weddings and other social affairs; and the rooftop House of Nothing, an observation deck with a stunning view of Mount Fuji.

223

HOUSE OF NOTHING AXONOMETRIC

The House of the Blue Shadow (opposite), clad in oxydized brass, stands in the south garden and is used for large communal gatherings. The rooftop House of Nothing (above) is an observation deck offering spectacular views.

The overall project design is unusual for the Japanese, in not only form but content: after all, the construction of individual houses—in or out of multiple housing complexes—is less common today in Japan than in America. The developers took a chance investing in this complex, but the risk has paid off: the project has been enormously popular. In Makuhari, art has dissolved several boundaries. ∎

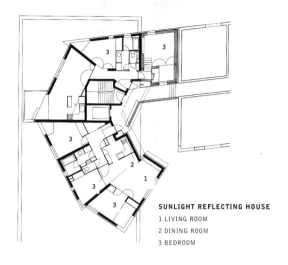

SUNLIGHT REFLECTING HOUSE
1 LIVING ROOM
2 DINING ROOM
3 BEDROOM

The Sunlight Reflecting House, a penthouse apartment, straddles two heavyweight buildings to form a roof over the east entrance to the complex.

JOHN LAUTNER ARCHITECT

GOLDSTEIN RESIDENCE
BEVERLY HILLS, CA

John Lautner entered the world of architecture in 1933 as an apprentice to Frank Lloyd Wright. After six inspiring years at Wright's Taliesin studio in Wisconsin and Taliesin West in Arizona, Lautner left to practice on his own in Los Angeles until his recent death. Lautner's architecture can be seen as a hybrid of Wright's approach and Lautner's own delight in technological daring. To some of the qualities he shared with his master—his gutsy individualism, his love of free-flowing, often angular spaces, his consistency between over-all concept and detail, and his wish to fuse building and nature—Lautner added an enthusiasm for the tools and gimmicks afforded by science. He especially loved poured concrete, which manages to be earthy even as it takes on daring futuristic forms. While he designed a number of bold and much-admired coffee shops for Los Angeles's automobile-dominated strips, Lautner is best known as a residential architect. The house he designed in 1963 for the Sheats family is an excellent example of his work, and has been remodeled by Lautner in recent years for its new resident, James Goldstein.

The living-room wing of the house is covered by a wide, waffle-gridded concrete roof folded down on two sides, which creates a cavelike lair from which to oversee the lights of the city. To maintain an uninterrupted view and a continuous relationship with nature, to allow no division between house and pool, and to embody the easy life in California's balmy clime, the living room was originally designed without exterior walls, the internal environment modulated only by a forced air current at the perimeter. Hundreds of upturned water glasses were cast into the con-

The waffle-gridded concrete roof soars above the living room, which is divided almost imperceptibly from the pool terrace by a suspended frameless glass wall.

crete roof, allowing sunlight to flicker down into the room.

James Goldstein bought the house in 1972 and, in 1980, began altering it with Lautner's help. In every case, the changes employed new technical systems or improved materials to further the design's original premise, to create an unfettered flow between building and nature.

To keep the living room open to the view, though no longer open to the air, Lautner used half-inch tempered frameless glass to replace a steel-framed window wall built by an owner subsequent to the Sheats. Skylights over the newly furnished kitchen and dining area were enlarged and fitted with motors so that they could retract, permitting cooking and eating under the open sky. Plaster walls were rebuilt in concrete, plaster ceilings were reclad in redwood, and glazed walls were upgraded with tempered glass. Concrete seating, tables, and bookshelves were added to the living room, all in keeping with the triangular shape that is the basis of the plan of the house. Additional changes—a concrete terrace, tropical gardens, an office—continue to be executed by former colleagues and members of the John Lautner Foundation, following the designs or the spirit of Lautner.

The angularity of the scheme is apparent everywhere in the architecture and the furniture, as seen in the living room (left above), kitchen (right top), and walkway to the master bedroom suite.

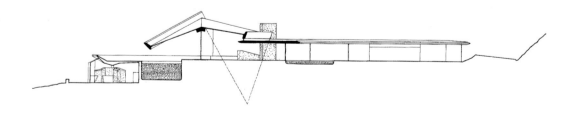

Upturned drinking glasses were cast into the living room's concrete roof to allow sunlight to filter down (opposite). In the living room as in the master bedroom (above) much of the built-in furniture is concrete.

232

One of the most dramatic alterations was made by Lautner in 1991. The master bedroom, located beneath the pool terrace, was reconfigured. Several small rooms were combined into one large bedroom/media room, with the focus on the view to the south. At the southern prow-shaped corner, two glass walls slide back at the touch of a button to create a breathtaking, vertiginous deck. Not to be outdone in its daring, the master bathroom is wholly glazed along its exterior perimeter. The glass sink itself is an elegant sculpture and inside-to-outside waterfall. Here, once again, Lautner dissolved to the utmost the visual boundaries between building and nature while gleefully exploiting technology. ■

Glass walls reveal spectacular views of nature and the city in the distance. At the room's acute-angled corner (opposite), the glass can retract to create a spectacular deck.

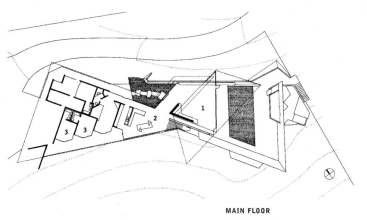
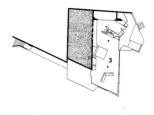

MAIN FLOOR
1 LIVING ROOM
2 DINING ROOM
3 BEDROOM

LOWER FLOOR
3 BEDROOM

The master bedroom's unique details include windows in the side of the pool itself (above left) and an all-glass sink from which water drains to the outside.

PROJECT AND PHOTOGRAPHY CREDITS

PACIFIC PALISADES RESIDENCE, PACIFIC PALISADES, CA

Architect: Gwathmey Siegel & Associates Architects, LLC, New York. Charles Gwathmey, principal. Gerald Gendreau, associate-in-charge

Consultants: Spindler Engineering Corp. (civil); Severud Associates (structural); The Sullivan Partnership (mechanical); Athans Enterprises, Inc. (electrical); Construction Specifications (specifications); Hillmann DiBarnardo & Associates (lighting); Precision Projection Enterprises (screening room); Burton & Co. (landscape); Guggenheim Asher Associates (art); Charles Salter Associates (acoustical); Sound Solutions (systems integrator); Isfahani & Phillips/NI Design (storage)

General contractor: ARYA

Photography: © Assassi Productions

STREMMEL HOUSE, RENO, NV

Architect: Mack Architects, Venice, CA. Mark Mack, principal; Robert Flack, project architect; Tim Sakamoto, Gloria Lee, project team

Client: Pete and Turkey Stremmel

Consultant: Parker Resnick, engineer; Terry Hunzinger, interiors

Photography: © Richard Barnes

BARRY'S BAY COTTAGE, ONTARIO, CANADA

Architect: Hariri & Hariri, New York. Gisue Hariri, Mojgan Hariri, principals in charge. Paul Baird, Graydon Yearick, Brigid Hogan, Aaron McDonald, design team

Client: Jane Baird and Dr. Charles Baird

Consultants: Robert Silman Associates, P.C. (structural); P.J. Stringer Surveying Ltd. (surveyors); Paul Walkington (geotechnical); M.W. Swinarski (associate architect)

General contractor: Zuracon Inc.

Photography: © John M. Hall

PARK ROAD HOUSE, TORONTO, ONTARIO

Architect: Donald McKay and Company, Ltd., Toronto. Donald McKay, designer; Douglas Birkenshaw, Tim Boyd, Janine Debanne, John Filipetti, Bruce March, Sarah Pearce, Mark Pitman, John Potter, Michael Wabb, project team

Client: Sandra Simpson

Consultants: James Floyd & Associates (landscape); Peter Sheffield & Associates (structural); Trinh Engineering (mechanical); Tanco Engineering (electrical)

General contractor: Marcus Design Build

Photography: © Robert Burley, Design Archive Inc.

COLLECTIVE HOUSING, MENDOCINO COUNTY, CA

Architect: Fernau & Hartman, Berkeley, CA. Richard Fernau and Laura Hartman, principals-in-charge; David Kau, Tim Gray, Kimberly Moses, Emily Stussi, project team

Client: seven households from Northern and Southern California

Consultants: Dennis McCroskey (structural); William Mah (mechanical); Zieger Engineers (electrical); John Furtado (landscape)

General contractor: Jim Boudoures

Photography: © Richard Barnes

LANDES HOUSE, GOLDEN BEACH, FL

Architect: Carlos Zapata Design Studio, Miami Beach. Carlos Zapata, John West, Catalina Landes, design team; Eduardo Calma, Maria Wilthew, Frank Gonzalez, Jose Rodriguez, Claudia Busch, design contribution; Melissa Koff, project coordinator; Una Idea, associate architect

Consultants: Leslie E. Robertson Associates: William Faschan, project engineer (structural); Lauredo Engineers (mechanical/electrical); Raymond Jungles Inc. (landscape)

General contractor: Cruz R. Rodriguez

Photography: © Peter Aaron/Esto Photographics

TEIGER HOUSE, SOMERSET COUNTY, NJ

Architect: RoTo Architects, Inc. , Los Angeles. Michael Rotondi, Clark Stevens, principals; Michael Brandes, Brian Reiff, Craig Scott, project team; Rebecca Bearss, Francisco Gutierrez, Lisa Iwamoto, Kenneth Kim, Tracy Loeffler, Donato Maselli, Stuart Spafford, assistants

Client: David Teiger

Site architect: Brandes:Masselli Architects. Michael Brandes, Donato Maselli, principals

Consultants: Douglas T. Lawton (owner's representative); Joseph Perazzelli (structural engineer); MB&A: Mel Bilow, Paul Ferbache (mechanical); G&W Consulting Electrical Engineers (electrical); Gladstone Design, Inc. (civil); Walter S. Carrell Jr., Inc. (landscape); Torsilieri, Inc. (site and landscape contractor); Brigitte Semtob, Ivan Chermayeff, Frank Maresca (art installation); Sandy Grotta, Brigitte Semtob (interiors); Fisher Marantz: Renfro Stone, Henry Forrest (lighting); Chermayeff & Geismar, Inc.: Tom Geismar (graphics); Pine Brook Cabinets (millwork); Franklin Central Communications (smart house); Fahy Electric, DeLucca Electric (electrical contractors); Charles Lehr (tile/stone); J.F. Lemmbeck, Inc. (masonry); Aileron Design, Red Hook Fabricators (architectural steel); Vulcan Supply Corp.: Larry Stearns (metal roof)

Contractor: F.J. Korfmann Contracting, Inc.

Photography: © Jeff Goldberg/Esto Photographics

CROFFEAD HOUSE, CHARLESTON, SC

Architect: Clark & Menefee Architects, Charlottesville, VA. W. G. Clark, Charles Menefee III, Daniel Stuver, William Vukovich, Robert Amerman, design team

Client: Dr. and Mrs. Thomas G. Croffead

Consultants: Dian Boone (interior design); Sheila Wertimer (landscape); Shoolbred Engineers Inc. (structural); Engineering Technology Inc. (mechanical)

Builder: Stier, Kent & Canady

Photography: © Timothy Hursley

MOUNTAIN HOUSE, DILLARD, GA

Architects: Scogin Elam & Bray Architects, Inc., Atlanta. Mack Scogin and Merrill Elam with Lloyd Bray, principals in charge; Denise Dumais, Kevin Cannon, Beth Morris, Kathy Wright, design team

Consultants: March Martin (landscape); Palmer Engineering Company (structural); Ramon Luminance Design (lighting); Waller Davis & Assoc. (hardware); Koets Corp. (kitchen); Parker Sales Co. (hydronic heating)

Builder: Winfred McKay

Photography: © Timothy Hursley

DAN HOUSE, MALIBU, CA

Architect: Israel Callas Shortridge Associates, Beverly Hills. Franklin D. Israel, principal in charge; Steven S. Shortridge, project architect; Fernando Bracer, Barbara Callas; Sigrid Geerlings; Austin Kelly; Michael Matteuci; William Molthen; Jefferson Schierbeek; Tom Zook, project team

Consultants: Stephen Perlof (structural); Roy McMakin (interiors); Jay Griffith (landscape); Future Home: Murry Kunis (audio/visual); Kitchens by Design: Don Silvers (kitchen); Fire L.T.D.: David Steinitz (lighting)

General contractor: Archetype: Larry Dubey, superintendent

Photography: © Erhard Pfeiffer

WHITE RESIDENCE, PINNACLE PEAK, AZ

Architect: Antoine Predock, Architect, Albuquerque, New Mexico. Antoine Predock, principal; Geoffrey Beebe, Ron Jacob, Jon Anderson, design team

Client: Originally commissioned by Gene and Donna Fuller; now owned by Richard and Patty White

Photography: © Timothy Hursley

KNEE RESIDENCE, NORTH CALDWELL, NJ

Architect: UKZ, New York. Simon Ungers, Laszlo Kiss, Todd Zwigard, principals. Adalbert Albu, associate architect

Client: Mr. Stephen and Mrs. Carole Knee

Consultants: Raymond A. Pasquale Associates (structural)

General contractor: CSR Construction Corporation

Photography: © Catherine Bogert

LAWSON/WESTEN HOUSE, LOS ANGELES, CA

Architect: Eric Owen Moss, Culver City, CA. Eric Owen Moss, architect. Jay Vanos, project associate. Todd Conversano, Jae Lim, Jennifer Rakow, Sheng-yuan Hwang, Scott M. Nakao, Dana Swinsky Cantelmo, Amanda Hyde, Elissa Scrafano, Augis Gedgaudas, Mark Lehman, Eric Holmquist, Sophie Harvey, Christine Lawson, Andreas Aug, Urs Padrun, Christoph Lueder, project team

Client: Linda Lawson and Tracy Westen

Consultants: Davis Design Group/Davis -Fejes Design: Greg Davis (structural); AEC Systems: Greg Tchamitchian (mechanical); Saul Goldin & Associates: Saul Goldin (lighting); Rolla J. Wilhite with Linda Lawson (landscape); Weiss Kitchens: David Weiss (kitchen); Farrage & Co.: Tom Farrage (furniture/fixture fabrication); HTS Architectural Interiors (interiors)

Contractor: Admiral Construction: John Blackley

Photography: © Scott Frances/Esto Photographics

GROTTA HOUSE, HARDING TOWNSHIP, NJ

Architect: Richard Meier & Partners, Architects, New York. Richard Meier, Michael Palladino, design team; David Ling, associate-in-charge; Charles Crowley, Christian Hubert, Lucy Kelly, Ralph Stern, collaborators

Client: Mr. and Mrs. Louis Grotta

Consultants: Severud-Szegezdy (structural); John Altieri, P.E. (mechanical and electrical); Quennell-Rothschild (landscape architects)

General contractor: Drill Construction

Photography: © Scott Frances/Esto Photographics

BLADES RESIDENCE, SANTA BARBARA, CA

Architect: Morphosis, Los Angeles. Thom Mayne; principal; Kim Groves, Mark McVay, project architects; Erik Andersson, Frank Brodbeck, George Hernandez, Stephen Jones, Jun-Ya Nakatsugawa, Peter McGovern, Kinga Racon, Stephanie Reich, Mark Sich, Stuart Spafford, Patrick Tighe, William Ullman, assistants

Consultants: Joseph Perazzelli (structural); Mel Bilow (mechanical); David Inger (Title XXIV); John L. Burnaby (radiant heating); Ilya Magid (masonry)

Contractor: Kirk Lewis, Froscher Lewis

Photography: © Atelier Kim Zwarts

CONCORD HOUSE, CONCORD, MA

Architect: Machado and Silvetti Associates, Inc., Boston. Rodolfo Machado and Jorge Silvetti, designers; Peter Lofgren, architect; Douglas Dolezal, design coordinator; Elizabeth Gibb, Mark Schatz, assistants.

Consultants: Sarkis Zaroonian (structural)

General contractor: Kistler and Knapp Builders

Photography: © Peter Aaron/Esto Photographics (pages 160–63, 165–66, 168–69); © Eduard Hueber (pages 164, 167)

31ST STREET HOUSE, SANTA MONICA, CA

Architect: Koning Eizenberg Architecture, Santa Monica, CA. Hank Koning, Julie Eizenberg, principals; Tim Andreas, project architect; Brian Lane, project team

Client: Joanne and Philippe Marill

Consultant: Ross Downey & Assoc. (structural)

Contractor: Charles Kuipers Design, Inc.

Photography: © Tim Griffith, Images Australia

TARZANA HOUSE, TARZANA, CA

Architect: Koning Eizenberg Architecture, Santa Monica, CA. Hank Koning, Julie Eizenberg, principals; Tim Andreas, project architect

Client: Bruce Shragg

Contractor: Roman Janczak

Photography: © Tim Street-Porter

HOFFMAN HOUSE EXPANSION AND RENOVATION, EAST HAMPTON, NY

Architect, Expansion and Renovation: Stamberg Aferiat Architecture, New York. John Schneider and Blake Goble, design team

Original House Architect: Richard Meier & Partners, Architects

Client: Anita Hoffman

Consultants: Robert Silman Associates: Nat Oppenheimer (structural); Jordan Fox, P.E. (mechanical)

General contractor: Joseph Chasas

Photography: © Paul Warchol (pages 184–87, 190–93); Ezra Stoller © Esto (pages 188–89)

SEADRIFT LAGOON HOUSE, STINSON BEACH, CA

Architect: Stanley Saitowitz Office, San Francisco. Stanley Saitowitz, principal in charge; John Winder, project architect; Daniel Luis, assistant

Client: Jim and Mary Lou McDonald

Contractor: Natoma Construction

Photography: © Richard Barnes

CASA LOS ANDES, LIMA, PERU

Architect: Arquitectonica International Corporation, Miami, FL. Bernardo Fort-Brescia and Laurinda Spear, principals and project designers; Martin J. Wander, project manager; Enrique Chuy, project coordinator; Bill Holt and Richard Perlmutter, design development

Consultants: Diar Ingenieros, S.A. (electrical); Gallegos-Rios-Casabonne-Uccelli-Icochea-Arango (structural); Dimonsa Ingenieros, S.A. (plumbing)

General contractor: G.L. Dupuy, Ingenieros

Photography: © Timothy Hursley

BERKOWITZ-ODGIS HOUSE, MARTHA'S VINEYARD, MA

Architect: Steven Holl Architects, New York. Steven Holl, Peter Lynch, project architects; Stephen Cassell, Peter Shinoda, assistants

Client: Steven Berkowitz, Janet Odgis

Consultants: Robert Lawson (structural); Alvin Cooke (custom steel and brass)

General contractor: Doyle Construction

Photography: © Paul Warchol

MAKUHARI HOUSING, CHIBA, JAPAN

Architect: Steven Holl Architects, New York. Steven Holl, principal-in-charge; Tomoaki Tanaka, project architect; Mario Godden, Thomas Jenkinson, Janet Cross, Terry Sujan, project team/master plan phase; Anderson Lee, Sumito Takashina, Sebastian Schulze, Gundo Sohn, Justin Korhammer, Bradford Kelly, Lisina Fingerhuth, Anna Mueller, Jan Kinsbergen, Hideaki Ariizumi, project team/design development, construction document phase

Associate Architects: Kajima Design; K. SONE + Environmental Design Associates

Consultants: Kouichi Sone (block design coordinator); Toshio Enomoto/Kajima Design (block architect); JUKA Garden and Architecture (landscape); L'Observatoire (lighting)

General contractor: Kajima+Kaisei+Mitsui JV

Photography: © Paul Warchol

GOLDSTEIN RESIDENCE, BEVERLY HILLS, CA

Architect: John Lautner, Architect, Los Angeles. John Lautner, principal-in-charge; Andrew Nolan, Helena Arahuete, and Strickland Nicholson Architects, project architects

Consultants: Andrew Nasser (structural); Eric Nagelmann (landscape)

Photography: © Alan Weintraub